Potty Training

An Essential Step-By-Step Guide to Having Your Toddler Go Diaper Free Fast, Including Special Methods for Boys and Girls

© Copyright 2020

The contents of this book may not be reproduced, duplicated or transmitted without direct written permission from the author.

Under no circumstances will any legal responsibility or blame be held against the publisher for any reparation, damages, or monetary loss due to the information herein, either directly or indirectly.

Legal Notice:

You cannot amend, distribute, sell, use, quote or paraphrase any part or the content within this book without the consent of the author.

Disclaimer Notice:

Please note the information within this document is for educational and entertainment purposes only. No warranties of any kind are expressed or implied. Readers acknowledge that the author is not engaging in the rendering of legal, financial, medical or professional advice. Please consult a licensed professional before attempting any techniques outlined in this book.

By reading this document, the reader agrees that under no circumstances are is the author responsible for any losses, direct or indirect, which are incurred as a result of the use of information contained within this document, including, but not limited to, —errors, omissions, or inaccuracies.

Contents

INTRODUCTION 1
CHAPTER ONE: WHEN TO START POTTY-TRAINING 3
    TODDLER DEVELOPMENT AND POTTY-TRAINING... 6
    SIGNS THAT YOUR TODDLER IS READY FOR POTTY-TRAINING....................... 11
CHAPTER TWO: POTTY-TRAINING MYTHS AND MISCONCEPTIONS 14
CHAPTER THREE: DITCHING DIAPERS (WITHOUT THE DRAMA) 22
    CHOOSING THE RIGHT POTTY GOES A LONG WAY.. 23
    LET'S GET RID OF THE DIAPERS.. 24
    SOME DO'S AND DON'TS... 25
    SOME TECHNIQUES TO HELP YOUR CHILD DITCH THEIR DIAPERS WITHOUT THE DRAMA.. 29
CHAPTER FOUR: POTTY-POOPING PSYCHOLOGY AND MENTAL PREPAREDNESS 31
    MENTALLY PREPARING YOUR CHILD FOR POTTY-TRAINING 31
    WHY YOUR CHILD'S HAVING A HARD TIME POTTY-TRAINING 32
    PSYCHOLOGICAL EFFECTS OF BOTCHED POTTY-TRAINING 38
CHAPTER FIVE: USING THE POTTY FOR THE FIRST TIME 40
CHAPTER SIX: POTTY AND POOPING PROBLEMS 49
    HOW YOU CAN SOLVE SOME OF THESE POTTY-TRAINING PROBLEMS 54

CHAPTER SEVEN: NIGHTTIME POTTY TRAINING 58
  DIFFERENCE BETWEEN DAYTIME AND NIGHTTIME POTTY-TRAINING 58
  WHEN TO START NIGHTTIME POTTY-TRAINING 59
  HOW LONG DOES NIGHTTIME POTTY-TRAINING LAST? 60
  TIPS YOU CAN FOLLOW 61
CHAPTER EIGHT: POTTY TRAINING GIRLS VS. BOYS 66
  TEN GENDER-SPECIFIC TIPS TO HELP YOUR TODDLER 69
CHAPTER NINE: FORMING POTTY HABITS 76
CHAPTER TEN: FROM POTTY TO ADULT TOILET 84
  THE RIGHT AGE TO TRANSITION TO THE TOILET 86
  TIPS TO MAKE THE TRANSITION EASIER 87
CONCLUSION 90

Introduction

Do you want to potty-train your child but don't know where to start? Well, say goodbye to all your worries. In this book, we shall discuss every single facet of potty-training in a very thorough manner. We will be covering every single base that concerns the training process, from picking the right time to potty-train your toddler to ditching diapers in a hassle-free way.

The book explores ten topics that revolve around potty-training that will make the entire process easier on your nerves, manageable to your schedule, and easy for your child.

When is the right time to potty-train? Is there such a thing as potty-training your child too early? Too late? What are signs that they are ready for potty-training? How should you start their training?

Then, we'll bust myths that surround potty-training, such as early potty-training can cause bladder damage. Spoiler alert, there's no truth to it. We'll discuss a total of sixteen of these myths before moving on to how you can get your toddler to bid adieu to diapers.

We'll further delve into the psychology of potty-training and how a botched training can result in lasting psychological damage to your child.

How should you make your child use the potty for the first time? Which is the better option for them, the potty, or the toilet seat?

We'll also expound on the problems that may arise in the potty-training process.

Did you know that there's a marked difference between daytime potty-training and nighttime potty-training? The biggest difference is the child's development. We'll elucidate how to go about nighttime potty-training and the precautions to take.

Is potty-training a boy different from a girl? Yes. The eighth chapter covers those differences.

What is a surefire way to build your child's potty habit? We shall talk about methods that embed this habit in their little minds, making them stick to a routine throughout the day, and eventually, throughout their lives.

Last, this book involves the transition from potty to an adult toilet and what the transition entails.

If those points and questions mentioned above have occurred to you throughout your child's training, buy this book and read it cover to cover! It contains thoroughly researched, fact-checked, concise information that shall make you a potty-training expert in a matter of a few hours.

From step-by-step instructions to succinct bullet points, this book is written in a casual, friendly, and easy-to-comprehend way that helps you understand the training process deeply and clearly. We have left no stone unturned in this guide to getting your toddler diaper-free.

Potty-training a child is no easy feat. It's one of the biggest challenges a parent can face in their child's development. We have meticulously rooted out every single aspect of the training and explained it in an intuitive manner that will be beneficial for you and your toddler.

Chapter One: When to Start Potty-Training

Potty-training is an important milestone for you and your child, with its success depending on several factors such as the physical, mental, behavioral, and developmental changes in your child's life rather than just their age. However, most children display signs they are ready for potty-training somewhere between the ages of 18 months to 24 months. This is not a hard and fast rule, though, as some children might not display those signs before they are at least 3 years of age.

To ascertain if your child is ready for potty-training or not, ask yourself these questions:

- Is my child able to walk to the toilet and sit on it?
- Is my child able to pull their pants up and down?
- Does my child stay dry for longer spells, such as two hours?
- Is my child able to comprehend and follow my instructions? (Basic instructions; not advanced tasks)
- Does my child convey the need to go to the toilet verbally and non-verbally?

- Does my child appear to be interested in going to the toilet?

If most answers to those questions were yes, your child is probably ready to start potty-training. If most answers to those questions was no, then it might be better to wait.

Although it is agreed that the best time to start potty training is when your child shows signs of readiness, but another readiness must be accounted for: yours. Instead of appearing too eager for the training to your child, let them, with their own motivation, take the lead. Another thing to remember here is that your child's success or difficulty in the potty-training does not connote to their intelligence. And since this is a training process, they will inevitably make mistakes and make accidents throughout. This does not call for punishment. There is no room for punishment in the potty-training process.

Here, I summarize the series of steps you can follow to make sure things go smoothly after you have determined that your child and you are ready to begin potty-training:

1. Pick Out Positive Reinforcement Phrases

Choose a selection of words to say to your toddler when referring to their potty-training. Positive reinforcement goes a long way in making them feel encouraged and involved in the process. When referring to their bodily fluids, such as their urine and their poop, avoid using negative phrases such as "made a stinky" or "dirtied your pants." This will make them associate the activity as something shameful or reprehensible, which will put them off from their training.

2. Make Sure All the Equipment is Prepped in Advance

We're talking about potty chairs and stools in the bathroom so that when they visit the toilet, they can easily prop themselves up on the stool and sit on the potty chair. Have them take a dry run (with their clothes still on) on the chair to acquaint them with it. Ask them how it feels. Have them put their feet on the stool to make them comfortable while sitting on the chair. Again, use positive phrases for the toilet.

You can show them the purpose of the toilet by emptying a dirty diaper in it and asking them to flush it.

3. Keep a Schedule

Schedule regular potty breaks, such as in the morning right after they wake up and after every nap they take. In addition, schedule a break every two hours and make them sit on the toilet (or potty chair) with no diaper. With boys, have them practice peeing sitting down on the toilet first. Then, once they have mastered that, show them how to do it while standing up. During your child's scheduled potty breaks, accompany them and either talk to them or interact with them by playing with a toy or reading them their favorite story.

4. Respond Quickly

Take your child to the toilet immediately when you see the signs such as squatting, grunting, squirming, wincing, and grabbing their genital area. Your quick response will help them associate their discomfort with the need to go to the toilet. Praise them throughout, such as telling them they did well to tell you they had to go to the toilet. While potty-training your child, you should keep them in comfortable, loose clothes, so there's less hassle for both them and you in terms of removing them.

5. Teaching Them the Hygienic Way

Explain basic hygiene to your child, such as wiping with toilet paper once they are done. For girls, you must teach to wipe front to back (up to down) so they prevent any germs and fecal particles from making their way to their bladder or vagina. Instruct your child they must always wash their hands afterward. Once you have covered the basics, tell them they have to flush the toilet and put the lid down.

6. Bid Adieu to the Diapers

Once you and your child have progressed past the first few weeks of this critical process, it's time to ditch the diapers in favor of underwear or training pants. This is a big step for both of you, and it's recommended that you celebrate it with them. However, if you feel they cannot stay dry, you can revert them to diapers. There's no rushing this final leg of the process.

What if they are not getting the hang of it?

If you feel like your child is having difficulty in staying dry or that they cannot stick to the schedule, maybe they are not ready for potty-training yet. You can try again in a few months. If, however, you notice they aren't ready and, despite that, try to force them to acclimatize, it may backfire on you. You don't want to create a power struggle or make them rebel. Both of you are on the same team here.

What do I do when accidents happen?

Accidents will happen. When they do, do not scold your child, do not discipline them by way of punishment, and, most important, do not guilt-trip or shame them. Staying calm and remaining positive will go a long way in making sure that they don't repeat the mistake.

Keep diapers, a change of clothes, and extra underwear on hand, so that when or if an accident happens, you can quickly change their clothes, especially in a daycare or school setting.

Toddler Development and Potty-Training

Before establishing the appropriate time for starting potty-training, let us look at the development stages of a child. According to the Nemours Foundation, there are six stages of your child's development. They are:

1 Year (12 Months)

Your baby is a toddler now. They will walk soon if they haven't already. They will explore previously unexplored areas, becoming freer in their locomotion and interaction with the environment.

In terms of communication, they will point to things and vocalizing their recognition, they will wave hello and goodbye, they will babble so it mimics talking. Most important, they will call you and your partner by "mama" and "papa."

About movement, your toddler will stand on their own, walking with either one hand held or alone, play with toy cubes and shapes and bang them together, be able to grip things with their full hand and use their hands to pick up chunks of food to bring to their face during mealtimes.

They will enjoy games like peekaboo. They will enjoy story time, being read to, and looking at bright, vivid pictures in picture books. They will express displeasure when you leave the room by way of crying. They will feel happy and become gleeful when they accomplish something new, such as walking a relatively longer distance, creating a tower of blocks, or succeeding in a simple game.

Cognitively, they can follow simple commands, imitate their elder siblings and parents, and be able to turn the pages of a book to picture that they like better than the others. They will also vie for your attention by doing something like dropping their toy, wailing, or laughing.

15 Months

At this age, your toddler will become more expressive about their wants and needs. However, their increasing capacity for the verbal enunciation of what they want (such as their pointing to an object and making a sound) means they will also throw tantrums when they don't get their way. While dealing with their tantrums, realize that they are an essential and very normal part of your child's development. You can distract them from their tantrums by indulging them in a game. And at the very least, you, being the adult, can keep calm when they're throwing a tantrum.

Communicatively, they will indicate their want by pointing at something, pulling at it, or grunting loudly. They will bring you their favorite book to be read or their favorite toy to play with. They will, besides saying "mama" and "papa," pick up a few new words and use them properly. If you playfully ask them, "where are your ears?" they can point to their body parts.

They will take more steps without your support. They can squat if they want to pick up something. they will be able to drink from a cup or a glass. They can stack toy cubes and doodle on paper with coloring pencils and crayons.

They will exhibit preferences for certain activities over others. They will use blankets, comforters, and teddy bears or other stuffed animals for self-comfort. They'll be better able to show their affection for you or a caregiver by kissing and hugging. Their dislikes, for things such as loud noises, will become more expressive.

Your child will understand simple commands and may follow them, depending on the mood they're in. They'll start mimicking what you do around the house, such as reading a book or watching TV. Around this time, it would be best to introduce them to problem-solving games, such as jigsaw puzzles.

1.5 Years (18 Months)

Around the time they're 1-1/2 years old, your toddler's growth will have slowed down a bit as compared to their first year of development. That is because babies grow at a faster rate than toddlers. Even though it will appear that their physical growth has somewhat decelerated, your child is still learning so much every day in terms of language, coordination, and balance.

An 18-month-old toddler can pronounce 10 to 20 words clearly. They will understand and respond to simple, one-step commands such as "Please pick your toy up." They will recognize and point to their body parts when asked.

They'll be able to run, climb the stairs with some assistance, take their clothes off, throw a ball, and scribble with their coloring pencils and crayons.

They'll start engaging in pretend play and will laugh when others laugh. They will be better able to show affection and will form the coordination skills required to play with other children. And they will show their irritation through tantrums.

At this age, they can name their toys, or at least their favorite ones, name and point at familiar imagery in their favorite picture book. They can imitate you by mimicking you sweeping the floor, cooking in the kitchen or talking to someone on the phone. They'll be able to match a pair of similar objects.

2 Years (24 Months)

This is the ideal time when potty-training comes into play. You can pick up on your child's cues, such as their interest in going to the toilet on their own, displaying signs they know the need to go to the toilet, and expressing their need to you.

In terms of communication, your child can now say 50 words or more. They'll be able to form basic sentences, sentences that even a stranger can comprehend. They'll use real words instead of made-up baby words, like calling "breakfast" breakfast instead of, say, "num-num."

They'll be able to run better, play with a ball by kicking or throwing it, walk up and down stairs without assistance (but please make sure to supervise them as they do so), be able to basic shapes, and sometimes they'll be able to feed themselves when food is put in front of them.

While previously they'd been able to follow one-step commands, now they'll be able to follow two-step commands, such as "Please pick your toy up and bring it to me." They'll grow more aware of their body and will be able to name more of their body parts. They'll engage in play-time with their toys more interactively, like feeding their teddy bear or doll or mimicking taking care of it like it was their baby.

2.5 Years (30 Months)

The most pronounced growth of your toddler at this age is in their vocabulary. They can now say more than a few hundred words. You can cultivate their sense of vocabulary by teaching them nursery rhymes, playing songs, and reading books to them.

They can speak phrases that comprise of three to four words. Other people can understand them more than half the time. They'll start using pronouns and they'll ask questions along the "what?" and "where?" lines.

They'll be able to wash their hands, dry their hands, brush their teeth with some assistance, pull their pants up, jump when they're joyful, and throw a ball with their hand.

In terms of social and emotional development, they'll participate in pretend play and enjoy it. They will participate in playing with other kids more proactively. They can tell you when they need to go to the toilet or when they need a diaper change. They'll be able to refer to themselves by their name.

Cognitively, they'll develop their sense of humor. Silly stories and funny baby jokes will appeal to them and make them laugh. They will understand the concept of things and items.

3 Years

When they are three years old, your toddler's imagination will soar. As a result, they'll start taking part in more make-believe games. But sometimes, their imagination will get the better of them and scare them. Benign shadows may appear as evil entities and spook them out. During this phase, listen to your child and reassure them.

In terms of language skills, they'll be able to form sentences with three or more words. You'll be able to understand what they're saying most of the time. This is an inquisitive age, at which they'll ask, "why?" a lot.

They'll be able to walk up and down the stairs with their feet alternating. When playing with a ball, they'll be able to catch it with both their hands. They'll try to balance on one foot and succeed sometimes. They'll be able to dress and undress with your assistance.

At this age, they will be potty-trained for the daytime. If they have a friend, they'll be able to refer to them by name. They'll also start identifying gender and begin referring to people as "him" or "her." They will also start to develop a sense of turn-based games, where they'll wait for their turn.

So, when should you start potty-training?

The best time to start training your child is when they begin showing signs that they are ready.

Children are unable to start using the toilet until they are somewhere between 18 months and three years. Girls are quicker to adapt to this than boys. Most parents will start training their children somewhere between two to three years.

Some parents follow a method called elimination communication, where they potty-train their child as young as four months. They will take their child immediately to the toilet when they see signs that they're about to pee or poop. Professionals do not recommend this method. It has been shown to cause complications later in life, such as difficulties when using the toilet in a public place like school.

It's also crucial to note that toddlers cannot control their bladder and their rectal muscles until they're at least 18 months year old. Therefore, it is important to wait for signs that they are ready to start potty-training.

Signs That Your Toddler is Ready for Potty-Training

Previously, we discussed some developmental milestones at various ages of your toddler. Those skills are somewhat of a prerequisite to their potty-training. As with other skills such as sitting up, crawling, walking, potty-training is an acquired skill and is best taught when your child's development (emotional and physical) is passed a certain point.

The key for potty-training is your child's desire for control, independence, self-mastery, and approval, i.e., their emotional readiness. Starting their potty-training before your child is ready can cause frustration on both ends.

Here are signs that you should look out for to gauge if your child is ready or not:

1. They begin Displaying Interest

When your child takes a keen interest in staying dry, staying clean, that's when you start potty-training them. Other signs of their interest to look out for are their piqued curiosity when you go to the toilet and their interest in wearing "big kid" underwear as opposed to diapers.

2. They Stay Dry for Longer Spells

If your child can stay dry for at least two hours, it's a sign that their bladder capacity has increased, which shows they are ready for potty-training.

3. They Know When They Go

After your child has done a number one or two in their diaper, they'll start showing signs like hiding behind the curtains or the furniture. They'll probably go to another room to poop or pee. That's another sign that signifies that they are recognizing when they are going. Training your child before this time will likely cause complications, as your child will not be aware of when they are going, and since they won't know it, they won't be able to understand it.

4. They Exhibit Independence

Look out for phrases such as "I can do it myself, mommy!" These cues signify a desire to become more independent, which is an important milestone for potty-training. However, if they're not ready, such as when they're going through stress (adapting to a newborn) or change (moving to a new house), it's better to delay the training till both you and the child are back to being comfortable.

5. They Can Take Their Clothes Off

Your child should be able to pull their pants up and down. While they didn't have a reason to do this in the past, now they do. It's an acquired skill, one of many during the potty-training process, and you should make it easier by dressing your child in loose, easy to take off clothing. Avoid clothes like rompers, tights, pants with zippers or belts, and any tight clothes that they'll have difficulty taking off.

6. They Can Follow Your Directions

Going to the toilet poses as challenges for your child, these challenges being: finding the toilet, turning on the bathroom's light, pulling down their pants, using a stool to get on the potty/toilet, relieving themselves, using toilet paper to wipe themselves, flushing, and last, washing their hands. If they're able to follow your directions with potty-training, they are ready to begin.

7. They Can Sit Still

Potty-training requires patience on the child's part. If they can sit still for extended periods without getting irritated, they can do so on the potty too.

8. They Can Walk and Run

If your child cannot walk or run properly, they aren't yet ready to start potty-training, as a major component of the training relies on them rushing quickly to the toilet whenever they feel like they have to go.

Chapter Two: Potty-Training Myths and Misconceptions

The territory of potty-training is riddled with myths and misconceptions. These are propagated by everyone from Cathy next door to some shady newsletter you keep getting in your email; all because of that one time you accidentally fed your address to some website offering you 20% off all baby clothing from their store. Separating fact from fiction is critical here because believing the myths and carrying them out will do you and your child more harm than good. Remember what Gandhi said, "Don't believe everything you read on the internet." Let's discuss some common myths and disprove them while we are at it.

1. Potty-Training too early will cause Complications like Constipation

You might have heard this one before from "veteran" parents now on their third or fourth child. Facebook mom groups and other social media platforms perpetuate that early training will cause your child to withhold, refuse to the toilet, and damage them psychologically. This is simply not true.

It does not depend on when you start the training as much as it depends on how you train them. If your approach to their training is gentle and makes sure that it keeps with the child's pace, no problems will occur. Scientifically, there is no connection between early potty-training and these issues. But there's research that states that early potty-training helps reduce the risk of toileting refusal, stool holding, and constipation.

Another research highlights the benefits of early potty-training, stating that infants can be potty trained by as early as 12 months if the training is done gentle and keeps the child's natural instincts in consideration. The child can go to the toilet independently by the time they're 24 months old.

Some things harmful to your child include punishing them, forcing them to push, and running the tap to hasten them. By including potty time in your child's routine early on, you can eliminate these aforementioned issues.

2. The Child has to be Ready before You Can Start Potty-Training

According to a study conducted by Douglas and Bloomfield in 1988, before the disposable diapers were invented—this is around the '70s—parents put their babies on potties right after they learned how to sit up, the babies, not the parents. Almost half of the babies, around the time they turned 12 months old, had stopped using diapers, and almost 80% were completely potty-trained by the time they were 18 months old. Other statistic-based research suggests that babies and toddlers are ready for and very much capable of potty-training when they reach 18 months and that the best time for ditching diapers is around 18 months to 30 months.

A pediatrician named Terry Brazelton developed the theory of "readiness" in the 1960s. Terry proposed this idea that children have to be ready before they're able to start potty-training. However, this theory, although it had some good ideas as its basis, was not sound, as most of the literature that Terry wrote was jarring and contradictory and missed major points about the child's development's in relation to potty-training commencement. Furthermore, Terry Brazelton was paid by Pampers to endorse their diapers. Many researchers say this made Brazelton turn his research into a marketing ploy to sell more disposable nappies, encouraging parents to let their children stay in diapers for longer to sell more Pampers rather than train their children.

The age that defines readiness for a child depends upon the skills they learn. These skills may be taught either socially or culturally. They need to have essential skills pre-developed, such as motor skills, to get trained. However, some parents do not consider these prerequisites and instead instruct their toddlers earlier than the recommended time.

3. The Bladder Gets Damaged Due to Early Potty-Training

As with other myths, this is false. Regularly going to the toilet protects your child's urinary bladder rather than damage it. By making them go to the toilet regularly, you help develop your child's sphincter control from a very early age. Training your child between the ages of 15 months to 24 months reduces the risk of bladder damage and bladder infection. It also reduces the risk of their wetting the bed. It improves their bladder function.

The urinary bladder is a muscle, and like other muscles, using it regularly strengthens it. Using it consciously, such as in potty-training, strengthens it further and ensures the establishment of a messaging system between their bladder and their brain. This system ensures the development of control and awareness in your child. There's research-based evidence that infants have bladder control from their birth and that they can learn to coordinate their urination as early as 9 months.

All toileting problems arise from your child's holding their poop or their pee. These problems include accidents involving poop, urinary frequency, bed-wetting, and urinary tract infections. Early potty-training helps reduce the risk of these accidents, ensures good bladder coordination, reduces the chances of their contracting infections, protects the bladder, and promotes staying dry during the daytime.

4. It's the Child that Decides When Potty-Training Happens, Not the Parent

This is one of those myths that sound like they have an element of truth to them but are false, overall. Yes, it's better that you let the child be a bit eager before starting their potty-training, but that does not mean that the entire decision is in their hands. They're just a child. You're the parent. Brazelton's research proposed that the child must be ready before you start their training, but later, more recent research conducted by Berk in 1990 stated that the whole process of potty-training gets wrapped up faster when the parent takes the reins of the process. This means you devote specific portions of time in the day to make sure that your child puts in consistent effort in their training. Remember, their readiness is not an innate trait that will just manifest itself one day out of nowhere. Their readiness depends upon the parent introducing the concept of potty-training to them and easing them into it. Your child will be interested in potty-training only if you help instill that interest in them. They can go to the toilet on their own only if you teach them the required skills.

If, however, you do follow that myth and let the child decide when they're ready, it will cause complications later on in their life. For example, introducing potty-training after your child is 24 months old will increase the risk of delayed bladder control and daytime wetting. Furthermore, if you delay it beyond the age of three years, it will create environmental, economic, and social complications.

5. Pull-Up Pants are Useful for Potty-Training

The entire marketing strategy behind pull-ups is that they're beneficial for potty-training. Here's how that's not exactly true. Pull-ups are a short-term comfort, both for the child and the parent. You as a parent, will be appealed by pull-ups avoiding potty-training accidents, such as leaking, bed-wetting, and so on. And you would be right to believe that. But here's the thing, pull-ups absorb the wetness, staying dry even after your child has urinated in them. In that regard, they work exactly like diapers. A research conducted by Rogers in

2002, states that because of that reason, pull-ups do not help in the potty-training process.

Another research study states that using pull-ups was less effective when trying to cultivate urinary consistency in a child.

While a child is a potty-training, they are essentially ditching an old way (the diapers) in favor of a new one. When you use pull-ups, you confuse the child by making them stick to the old way while also trying to teach them a new one. So, for the sake of the training, you shouldn't use pull-ups while potty-training your child.

6. Children Can Only Stay Dry Once their Hormones Have Developed

Okay. This one's a bit tricky, as hormones do play a factor in suppressing urine production. These hormones work for most children, but this doesn't mean that the myth is true. If your toddler or baby can stay dry during the day, thanks to your potty-training, they're likely to stay dry at night, despite whether their hormones have developed or not. This might surprise you, but if you've trained your baby from as early as six months, they'll be able to stay dry at night as they're no longer accustomed to the diaper.

7. Potty-Training Gets Done Quicker if You Start it Later

False! It takes the same time to potty-train a child early as it does later. Earlier, it's not recommended that you teach them potty-training after three years of age, because it will cause complications such as the increased risk for bed-wetting and soiling. The ideal time to start potty-training your child is between 18 to 24 months. Even if you take longer, such as after 25 months, it will take the same time. There's no rushing the process. There's no shortcut that will allow you to do it quicker. It's going to take time either way. Earlier potty-training is related to your child's acquiring urinary confidence, and not because of bladder dysfunction. If your child uses the potty early, they will develop that confidence and will ask you to take them to the potty sooner.

8. It's Easier to Train Girls Than Boys

Here's another classic myth that is not grounded in truth, whatsoever. It takes the same time to train a boy as it does for a girl. It's not a gender-based skill. Whether you're training a boy or a girl, the potty-training process should remain the same. Most parents, under the impression that boys are harder to train than girls, complicate the process needlessly for their child. Don't do that. They're both equally able to learn potty-training at the same pace.

9. Placing the Child on the Potty Forcibly Will Train Them

Not even a little bit. It might backfire. It might cause them to throw tantrums and develop irritability. But one thing it won't do: train them. There's a ton of parents who still hold to this myth as fact. This is a major misconception that needs to be rooted out right away. Remember, if you force your child, you're going to cause them to fear the potty. You're going to make them reel at the sight of it. If you keep on doing that, it will become a power struggle that will end up in a fight, and we know how these fights play out. The parent has to give up at the end because frankly, there's not much you can do when your child is wailing non-stop.

What you can do to make the transition easier is to communicate with your child and allow them to learn the signs they need to go. Communicate with them about it. Once they're aware of these signs (the signs we discussed in the previous chapter), they'll come to you themselves. As opposed to something that they fear, potty-training will become something that they'll look forward to.

10. Daycare Will Take Care of My Child's Potty-Training for Me

Uh-uh. No sir. Most daycares will turn you down if you haven't trained your child on your own, and the ones that do accept your child, they'll teach them potty-training in a way convenient for the daycare staff, i.e., a method involving pull-up pants and taking them to the potty every few hours. They will botch the potty-training process and cause numerous complications you will be left to deal with. It will boggle your child, resulting in the potty-training process taking longer than usual.

11. There's a Right Age for Potty-Training

Have you seen that meme with the pirate going, "Yes, but actually no?" It holds true for this myth. There's a right window for potty-training, sure, but there's no such thing as the right age for potty training. We've discussed that window. It is 18 to 24 months. But some parents are under the notion they should get their children off diapers by the time they're x months old. They forget that every child develops at their rate, and no two children are the same. While in some culture potty-training commences as early as nine months, and with some parents, they don't even train their child until they are three years of age. It all hinges on when your child has developed complementing traits that go along with potty-training.

12. You Should Celebrate and Applaud Your Child the First Time They Use the Potty

While it may seem like sound advice, another myth needs to be busted wide open. By appearing too enthusiastic, you might end up doing one of two things:

    a) You'll make your child think that they accomplished a great feat and that they should always be applauded whenever they go to the toilet

    b) if your child is shy, it will make them avoid going to the toilet because they'll hate the confrontation and the celebratory nature of going to the toilet.

This does not mean you don't praise your child. You should, but without sounding too enthusiastic and eager. A simple "good job!" will suffice.

Similarly, using stickers and stickers and other methods of celebrating achievement will put too much pressure on the child to always perform so it warrants praise. They will become anxious with the pressure to perform.

13. Putting Underwear on Your Child Will Quicken the Process

It won't. It's going to make them feel feelings of failure when they'll eventually soil their underwear. It's going to make them feel shameful and confused. Only put underwear on your child once they're in the final leg of the potty-training process, not before.

14. It's Better to Have a Potty-Trained Child Than Have Them in Diapers

Enjoy the diapers while your child is still in them. Remember, once you've potty-trained your child, you must attend to them every time they need to go. This will be especially difficult when you're, say, traveling, and need to stop every time they have to go to the toilet. Keep diapers on hand for such occasions until your child can remain dry for longer periods. There's no rushing the process.

15. There's No Going Back Once You've Begun Potty-Training

It's not an irreversible process. Sometimes your child cannot grasp the fundamentals, and it will seem like they're not ready. Notice that cue. That's usually a sign you need to delay the training. Take a break of a few months and then start the training afresh. Your child is going through various developmental changes; changes will sometimes not coincide with their potty-training and make them uncomfortable and distressed.

16. Nighttime and Daytime Potty-Training Should be Taught at the Same Time

Nighttime potty-training is related to urine production, retention, and hormones. It's quite different from daytime potty-training. Daytime training is easier to pull off and thus should be taught many months before they're finally able for nighttime training. The two don't go together.

Hopefully, covering these myths will help you differentiate between fact and fiction, thus easing the process both for you and your child.

Chapter Three: Ditching Diapers (Without the Drama)

Is there a right age to ditch diapers?

As we have previously discussed, there isn't just one right age to start your child's potty-training. Similarly, there's no right age to stop using diapers, as both these things—i.e., the potty-training and the diaper ditching—go in tandem. Some kids might be early adopters, while others might be late bloomers. However, is there such a thing as the right age to stop using diapers?

There's a window, a pretty long window, comfortable for both early adopters and late bloomers. It is 18 months to 3 years. That's when most children are capable of starting potty-training. Remember, the first step is getting them to use the potty. The diaper ditching comes way after that, once your child is comfortable going to the toilet on their own and are not wetting the bed at night.

Starting the diaper ditching process too early will only result in frustration for both you and your child, as most babies and toddlers cannot control their bowel and bladder before the age of 18 months. If you attempt to get them to ditch their diapers before that age, it will be unsuccessful. It might make the child feel rebellious, reluctant, and nervous about the whole potty-training process.

Second, there's the whole element of keeping backup diapers at hand to consider. If your child sees that you've kept spare diapers around and you use them whenever they're unable to go to the toilet, they'll stop taking the training seriously and fall back on the diapers, which is something that we do not want. Once you're past the first trimester of the training process, remove the diapers as an option so your child knows that the only way they can relieve themselves is by going to the toilet.

Third, you might be wondering how long the potty-training process will take. Again, it depends on the child. It might take as little as a week, or it might take many months. The duration of the potty training depends on several factors, including the child's age, their interest, and their development. If they are on the younger side, it will take them longer. Longer as in some weeks. If they are showing interest on their own, take that as a cue they are eager to do the process faster. That means that it will take them just a couple of days. If they are hesitant or resistant, they will take more time.

Last, even though it depends on the individual, the approximate duration for potty-training is between 3 to 6 months. If that makes you feel overwhelmed, don't worry. You just have to take it day to day, and before you know it, your child will be trained, and those diapers will be redundant.

Choosing the Right Potty Goes a Long Way

The next major step in ditching diapers is choosing the right potty for your child. Why? Because choosing the potty can make or break the process. If you pick one that your child takes to, it will catalyze the whole training process faster. They'll like using that potty and will prefer it to their diapers.

When you go on a shopping trip to choose the potty, take your child with you and involve them in picking their favorite one. Two kinds of potties are available in the market these days: the seat reducer and the stand-alone potty. The seat reducer is cheaper and doesn't take up as much space as the stand-alone potty. The seat reducer goes on top of the regular toilet seat and reduces the size of the ring to make it comfortable for your kid. One major advantage of the reducer is that it accustoms your child to the regular toilet much faster than the stand-alone potty. To use a stand-alone potty, your child will have an easier time going to the toilet by themselves, and you can have the main toilet in the house all to yourself.

When selecting a stand-alone potty, take into account these three things: the simplicity of the potty, the fit, and safety. For example, if your child's butt barely fits on the rim, they will feel very uncomfortable while sitting on it, which will set back the whole process. Then, make sure that you get the right size, meaning your child's feet can touch the ground when they're sitting on it. If you can get a potty that has handles on it, it will help your child maintain their grip while they're relieving themselves, which will be a major advantage.

If you are getting a potty for a boy, one thing to consider is if the potty has a splash guard or not. The splash guard, although not necessary, will make it easier to clean the potty, minimizing the mess. The splash guard should be just about high to help keep the pee inside the potty but not too high it makes peeing a difficult challenge.

The potty you choose must be easy to clean and simple to use. If you are shopping online for a potty, read the reviews to see what your fellow parents are saying about it.

Let's Get Rid of the Diapers

When you have bought your potty or seat reducer, the next step is to get rid of the diapers gradually. Doing it right away is ill-advised as the child has yet to get used to their new mode of going. Do it once they have gone to the potty at least ten to twenty times. Once they are used to the potty, make the diapers disappeared. It's tempting to keep them as a fallback, but in the long term, it will only serve to deter the potty-training process, and we don't want that.

Disclaimer: the transition from diapers to potty will cause some accidents, so brace for that. This will be frustrating at the moment but will ultimately make your child stick to the potty and not rely on diapers.

Remember, when your child has learned that they can relieve themselves by going to the potty, their instinct will want them to stay clean. Every time they get dirty (whether by accident or in transition), they will feel extremely uncomfortable. That uncomfortableness will quicken their adaption to the potty, as they will learn that the potty is the hassle-free way to go to the toilet without dirtying themselves.

Some Do's and Don'ts

Here are some do's and don'ts to follow as you are transitioning your child from diapers to potty.

1. Observe the signs that your child needs to go. These signs include squirming, grunting, fiddling with something in their hands, shuffling their feet, making faces, trying to communicate whether by verbal or non-verbal cues they need to go. Whenever you see these signs, rush your child to the potty. That way, you'll be able to avoid any accidents and acquaint them with the potty organically.

2. Do not force your child into potty-training just because they have reached a certain age. If you have more than one kid, you'll expect your toddler to learn at the pace your elder child learned. It's not the same for every child. While your elder child might have picked up on potty-training in a week or two, your toddler might not pick the habit that fast. Patience, as with other aspects of parenting, is key here.

3. We discussed dressing before, but it's so important that we will mention it again: dress your child in easy-to-take-off, loose clothes they can remove without a hassle whenever they need to go to the toilet. Overalls are a big no, with the exception that your child can very easily pull them off and put them back on without your help.

4. Do not listen to imposing relatives who pressurize you into getting your child out of diapers as early as you can. They are not there to deal with your child. Take their scolding advice and let it go from one ear and to the other one. If you feel overwhelmed by their advice, you will end up passing that tension to your child, making them feel stressed, which will set back the training.

5. Praise your child when they successfully go to the potty. But make sure not to go overboard with the praise, as it will make them associate praise with going to the potty, and they will start expecting it every time they use the potty. A simple pat or an encouraging phrase goes a long way in building their morale and confidence.

6. Do not engage in a battle of a power struggle with your child. Spoiler alert: They will always win. Why? Because while you have a rationale and logical thinking on your side, their trump card is irrationality and wailing and crying and throwing a tantrum. If they don't want to go, don't force them. Don't impose yourself on them needlessly. Pick your battles.

7. Let your child play with their favorite toy or read their favorite book to them while they are on the potty. If they get antsy when you're not there, keep them company as they go to the toilet.

8. Do not give nicknames to their body parts. Remember, we are trying to do the opposite of infantilizing them. Approaching the training in a matter of fact and logical manner will cultivate the importance of the process in them.

9. Let your child have autonomy when going to the toilet. The more independent they will feel, the quicker they can adapt to potty-training, and the quicker they'll ditch their diapers.

10. Do not punish your child if they make a mess when not in diapers. This will reinforce in their minds that using the diapers was a good thing, as they never got punished while using them, and that not wearing the diapers is a bad thing, as they got punished.

11. Criticizing your child's potty going methods will also complicate things for both of you. It will make you frustrated and it will take their confidence away.

12. Patience is the name of the game, and as clichéd as it sounds, it's true. Potty-training, and subsequently diaper ditching, is a time-consuming process that will test your patience at times, but remember that this is the first time your child is going through such a radical change. Keep reminding them gently that their poop and pee needs to go in the potty and not on the floor or in their clothes. Your attitude is contagious and will ultimately decide how the training turns out. If you are there for them, patiently reassuring them along every step of the way, you will make them independent faster. Remember that as hard as it gets for you, it's not easy for your child either. They have only just gotten control of their bladder and bowels, and now they're being trained for something they don't have a clue about. Empathize with your child, reaffirm their struggle, and occasionally cheer them on my celebrating minor milestones.

Is there any wisdom to potty-training boot-camps?

Yes. That might seem a very hot take on boot-camps, but here's the reason they're insanely popular: they work in a very short time, which is the entire point of a boot-camp. You devote an entire week to give your child a crash course of sorts in potty-training, at the end of which you have ditched their diapers and have shifted them permanently to the potty. There are various boot-camps, such as the three-day boot-camp, the five-day boot-camp, and the one-week boot-camp, all with the same goal: getting your child off the diapers.

But note that as appealing as it sounds, it will be grueling for you during the entire duration, as you will be expected to ditch all your tasks and focus solely on the boot-camp.

Let's Briefly Cover What Standard Boot-Camp Demands

Pick a weekend on which you're free and have no upcoming plans. Notice the signs that your child is ready, then begin. On the first day, i.e., Saturday, get your child off the diapers and introduce training pants in the mix. We talked about the disadvantages of the training pants, but here's the thing: that was for regular potty-training and not boot-camps. The rules for boot-camps are different and thus allow a little leeway for using training pants. So, on Saturday, put on training pants on your child. These are reusable and can be washed again.

Then on the same day, introduce them to the potty and see if they're up for it. If they do not feel intimidated by it, they can ditch the training pants and use the potty.

Tell your child to listen to the signs of their body and learn which signs connote to their need to go to the toilet.

This weekend, you will take your child to the bathroom when they wake up, before every nap, after every nap, before and after every meal, and before they go to bed. Besides all these scheduled visits, just make sure that they go to the toilet every two hours.

It's going to be a very rigorous routine for the three days of the boot-camp, but at the end of it, you're going to have a child who has learned how to use the potty and ditch their diapers.

Keeping Some Cleaning Supplies on Hand

Once you have gone to the diaper ditching route, make sure that you have cleaning supplies on hand because you will need them. Your child isn't expected never to make a mess. Between the transition from diapers to the potty, they will end up soiling their clothes or the house. But you'll be prepared for that. Stick up on the right cleaning supplies like Super-Sorbs for hard floors. They will soak up any pee, making it easier to clean. They can also absorb the smell, so you will have no rank smells coming from the floor after you're done cleaning. For other surfaces such as carpets or fabric, get something like Nature's Miracle or Rocco & Roxie. They're originally meant to be for pets, but many parents use them whenever some potty related accidents happen in the house. They can both remove stains and odors of pee and poop from the floors. Use nontoxic bleach for cleaning your child's underwear if they make a mess in them. For sanitizing surfaces, get disinfecting wipes that will clean up all the germs and fluids easily.

Some Techniques to Help Your Child Ditch their Diapers Without the Drama

Here are some parent-approved tips that will help your child transition to the potty with no fuss.

1. Turn the Training into a Game

There are ways to turn the potty-training routine into a game that your child actually looks forward to. Some parents put a Cheerio or a piece of Cheetos in the toilet and have their boy aim at it. This sparks their interest and makes them look forward to peeing in the toilet.

Some parents have tried putting food colors in the toilet so that whenever your child pees in it, the color changes, captivating their attention.

2. Turn Fear into Fun

Yes. Some children are afraid, and rightly so. Imagine it from their perspective. There's a big black hole in the toilet that they have to face every time they need to go. Some children might develop a phobia, while others will not think much of it. If your child shows signs they fear going to the toilet, it's time you swapped fear for fun by replacing their toilet with, say, a musical one. The musical toilet has a moisture activated sensor that plays nursery rhymes when the child pees or poops in it. If that doesn't help, keep them company and make their shift their focus from the toilet to you as you guide them and tell them not to be afraid.

3. Keep the Potty with You Wherever You Go

Whether you're sitting in the living room, the dining room, or the bedroom, take the potty with you wherever you and your child go.

Have them sit at the potty at regular intervals, even if they have to go or not.

4. Encourage their Efforts

Praising them on their successes is well earned and all, but also encourage them whenever they make an effort. Some of those efforts will cause them falling, some will cause them making a mess, but it will eventually lead them to become potty-trained, so whenever they make an effort, say something reassuring.

5. Ditching the Pants at Home

When your child is at home, try ditching their pants and letting them roam naked around the house. This, although it appears to be strange, will help them adjust to the potty by helping them become more aware of their body and easily going to the potty without the hassle of clothing in their way.

6. Charts and Stars are a No-Go

Chalk that up to going overboard with the process. It might help initially in terms of encouragement and reassuring them, but it will make them accustomed to getting a new star on their chart every time they go, and be frank with yourself, sometimes you just don't have the energy to put in the enthusiasm. What will happen then?

Chapter Four: Potty-Pooping Psychology and Mental Preparedness

Mentally Preparing Your Child for Potty-Training

Before you can actively train your child, you must prepare them mentally. The first thing you can do, an easy task that requires little mental and physical effort, is teaching them by example. Children are receptive to what their parents do. You might have seen their mimicking behavior around the house. Mimicking is one of their primary modes of learning. With potty-training, the mimicking translates to them seeing you going to the toilet and becoming intrigued about what you're doing in there. If you're worried about the image of you going to the toilet being burned in their mind such that they'll remember it when they'll have grown up, you can rest easy, as they won't be able to remember it. Do you remember things from back when you were 18 to 24 months old? No, right?

The next step is easier. Once they have seen you going to the toilet, explain to them what you are doing so that they can understand.

These include things such as removing your clothes while going to the toilet, flushing the commode, wiping, putting your clothes back on, washing your hands, and drying your hands. It'll get a little overwhelming for them if you try to explain it all at once, so be patient and take it one step at a time.

If the child sees the potty-training as something that they're already accustomed to, such as playing with their favorite toy or watching their favorite video on YouTube, they will be less daunted and more likely to look forward to going to the toilet. To that effect, make sure that at the beginning of the process, you have your child's potty somewhere familiar instead of the bathroom.

You can ask your child when they feel like their diaper is wet or full. Identify this behavior by asking them questions like, "Are you going to poop?" so your child can comprehend and recognize their urges to pee or poop.

Another thing you can do to prepare your child for potty training is keeping them in clean diapers. This requires you to be more attentive than usual, as you must replace their diapers within the window they dirty them. Once your child is accustomed to the feeling of cleanliness in their diapers, they will be mentally prepared to start potty-training.

Why Your Child's Having a Hard Time Potty-Training

It's crucial to understand that potty-training can be a very arduous task for your child, considering the number of changes they are going through. We are talking about their transition from diapers to the potty, their starting pre-school, moving from one place to the other, and learning all sorts of other things that aren't related to potty-training. This can overwhelm the child. It can cause unnecessary stress in their life. It might cause them to resist learning or straight up stop learning altogether. If your attempts at potty-training your toddler don't seem to work, here are reasons that will help you understand the why of it all. When you know the why, you can move on to the how. As in how to tackle those problems.

1. They are not Ready Yet

As much as we have discussed this, it needs to be reiterated at each stage of potty-training. Your child does not have control of their bladder and bowels before the age of 18 months, so teaching them potty-training before that time is not recommended. It will stall the progress and possibly cause complications that we shall discuss in the next section.

Listen, you might think that by putting your child on the potty every time they have to go—before they have turned 18 months old, that is—will train them, but it does not necessarily mean they are ready to go on their own. If you stop doing that, they will soil their diapers or pants. However, once after they've turned 18 months old, they will develop bladder and bowel control, and your training will pay off.

The not-being-ready-part is not limited to younger children. Sometimes, older children might have trouble because of being unready developmentally or medical issues, such as constipation.

Besides the physical and mental readiness, you must make sure that things are A-Okay at your house before you train them, specifically, in a familial capacity. Say you and your family are about to move, are planning to take a vacation or are about to have another baby. It might be better to wait because these changes signify new receptive learning for the child. When they are already too mentally occupied with other matters, it will not be the right time to potty-train them as their mental plates are already full.

Usually you can pick up on their lack of readiness through verbal and non-verbal cues. They will make faces, signifying displeasure and confusion and irritation, or they will tell you with their words and actions. If that persists, understand that they aren't ready and that they will be ready sometime later.

2. They Lack Interest

Think of the hundreds of different stimuli that your child is taking in at each moment. Imagine it from their perspective every little thing that their tiny little ears, ears, nose, mouth, hands, legs, and brain are witnessing, feeling, and assimilating. To say they are preoccupied with each of those stimuli wouldn't be an overstatement. We have to make a window for a teaching task, i.e., potty-training. If they do not pick up on it and instead give attention to other things, things such as the TV or their tablet or a gaming console, they are not to blame.

You are not to blame, either. This is a classic case of nobody's fault.

You have two options here. Either you can delay the potty-training till a time when they are less excited and antsy, or you can pique their interest in potty-training by including their favorite game, book, movie, or song in the mix. Understand that your child is not showing interest in the task because of some inborn rebellion or developmental disability; it's because there's too much going on their lives.

On a tangential note, the same goes for any other training. Whether you're teaching them how to speak, how to write, how to draw, or any other parental teaching task, if they cannot give their attention to the task at hand, it's because their little minds are overwhelmed with an overload of mental stimuli.

Some parents instruct their children in an environment where all other stimuli are zoned out, canceled. That's why they have a separate teaching room where there aren't any distractions. The same goes for potty-training.

3. They are Afraid of the Toilet

We've already covered this briefly, but now let's take another look from the perspective of your child having difficulty in adapting to potty-training. Your child knows when they are about to go to the bathroom. We discussed that. They will show their need to go either verbally or by nonverbal cues. So why would they rather dirty their diapers or their clothes instead of going to the bathroom? Well, it's because they're afraid of it. Again, it might be better to empathize and put yourself in your child's shoes. Look at the toilet. Look at it from their perspective. It's a huge porcelain chair with many moving parts, a huge height, and a giant hole in the middle, which flushes loudly. If they aren't afraid of the hole and the size, they might be afraid that they'll fall inside, and they'd be right to be afraid, as that has happened to many toddlers during their training. That's why it's recommended to use a training seat instead of just putting them on the plane seat.

Here are things that you can do to alleviate your child's fear of the toilet: Have them practice on the toilet by seating them on the toilet with their clothes still on. This way, you're familiarizing them with the toilet in a step by step manner. Put them on the toilet with the lid still on. This will help drive home the realization they aren't just going to fall inside. At this step, read their favorite book to them to distract them from the alien nature of the toilet. After your child can balance themselves on the closed toilet, you can lift up the lid and have them sit on it with their clothes on. Repeat that twice and then remove their clothes except the diaper. Last, have them sit on the toilet without the diaper and let them know that they have to go pee or poo. If your child resists at any step of the process, revert to the previous step so as not to overwhelm them.

This is why some parents prefer the potty to the toilet, as it helps familiarize the child without scaring them. Maybe your child fears the flushing of the toilet. There, you can explain to them the basics of how toilet plumbing works and demonstrate that working by having them flush a couple of toilet paper pieces.

4. They Do Not Want to Use a Public Toilet

This is a relatively rare case when you need to introduce your child to the public toilet, but since it happens lets cover it. Maybe you're traveling with your toddler and need to help them go to the toilet at a public toilet, or maybe they have to go to the toilet at their daycare or school. Regardless, sooner or later, your child must be introduced to the public toilet, which is a huge step for them, and as so, it will be scary for them. Scary as in they're afraid of the loud noises that emanate from the public toilet, noises such as the sound of flushing, people are talking, the hand dryer's loud whooshing, the opening, and closing of doors. While previously your child went to the toilet in the quiet comfort of their own home, now they're being made to go in a place that's altogether new and way too loud. Some public toilets have that auto-flush system, which can scare the child even more. If your child is resisting, it's recommended that you take a portable potty with you.

5. They are Anxious About Potential Accidents

This is a continuation of the last point. Suppose your child's potty-training is taking off at home, making you confident that they're able to use the toilet at a public place or at a friend or family member's home, and you introduce your child to a new toilet, you may notice that their displaying signs of nervousness. This is again due to the newness of the toilet. If the child is a little older, you can convey to them they can communicate their need to go, ask questions like "Where's the toilet," and express their need to go by saying, "I have to use the potty, please can you help me?"

Just in case, whenever you take your child out with you, pack a pair of clean clothes and diapers. This is for if or when they have an accident, you can help them regain their confidence by changing them into clean clothes quickly and letting them know that it's okay to have an accident.

6. They are Straight-Up Refusing to Potty-Train

Potty-training, both for you and your toddler, can be considered as the ultimate battleground. There are two methods of conflict. One's where you are pitted against your toddler, with the battlefield being that of potty-training. This is the bad kind of conflict. The other type of conflict, *the healthier one*, is where you and your toddler are in the same team, and potty-training's the opponent. In the former type of conflict, your child will become stubborn, and it will turn into a control issue.

Avoid that at all costs by being gentle with them and explaining it to them rationally that they can use the potty because now they are mature enough to do so. Be on their team; let them know that you're there for whenever they need assistance. Another thing you can do is provide them the illusion of control by giving them choices. Choose between two outfits, choose a TV program or a game on the tablet, choose what to eat, and so on. When they feel like they're somewhat in control, it will ease them into potty-training. It's vital to note there are three main things that your child can control: their need to eat and drink, their sleeping routine, and their toileting.

7. They Seem to be Slower than Your Other Child

We cannot stress enough that it is not a competition. Don't make it one. If your firstborn was quick to adapt to potty-train and your current child is seemingly having a tough time learning the ropes, it's not their fault. One method doesn't necessarily work for every child. Every child is different in their capacity to learn. One child may respond well to simple instructions; the other may respond well to rewards and positive affirmation.

Another significant difference that parents seem to overlook is the difference between potty-training boys and potty-training girls. Some boys are slower to adapt to potty-training than some girls. It's not always the case, but it's not unheard of either.

Every child develops at their own pace. It doesn't mean they lack or excel in terms of their intelligence.

8. Their Health Issues are Aggravating and Interfering

Constipation is often the culprit to difficulties in potty-training. When a child is constipated, they'll fear going to the potty because of the pain associated with passing stool. Longtime constipation can cause complications by putting stool pressure on the child's kidneys and bladder, making it painful for them and difficult for them to go to the toilet.

It can aggravate into chronic constipation, which can cause encopresis, in which the stool becomes backed up and clogged with stool, and so, liquid stool leaks out. If you notice your child making accidents with leaky poop, consult with a pediatrician.

Constipation can be treated by having your child drink more water, introducing vegetables and fruits in your child's diet, and using a mild laxative.

Constipation also contributes to irritation and loss of appetite, thus interfering in the potty-training process.

Psychological Effects of Botched Potty-Training

If you, as a parent, give in to stress, it can cause things to go awry, turning the critical process of potty-training botched. If you feel like stress is getting the better of you, you can step back and give yourself some me-time. Relax. Take a deep breath. Get back in there with a fresh mind, because if you give in to your stress, you might lash out at your child or beat them, and that can have long-lasting effects.

Child Abuse

The American Academy of Pediatrics states that more child abuse takes place during potty-training compared to other facets of the child's development. If you hit your child or punish them during their training, it will lead to emotional and mental scarring that will stay with them for the rest of their lives. It will manifest itself in suicidal behavior, violent behavior, withdrawn behavior, depression, and it will make them prone to substance abuse when they are older.

Putting Pressure on Them with Your Expectations

By pressuring your child to perform, you will not only delay their learning process but also make them anxious and fearful. This can lead to fecal affecting by making them withhold their stool out of nervousness and being scared.

Punishing Them for Accidents

Scolding your child or punishing them for something as natural as an accident will give them low self-esteem, make them doubt their selves, and make them feel ashamed and embarrassed. The embarrassment will, in turn, lead to them hiding their need to go to the toilet. Once a child has associated potty-training with feelings of fear and shame, they will avoid it.

Preparing Yourself for Potty-Training

To avoid botching their potty-training, realize that more than your toddler, it is you who need to prepare yourself mentally for potty training. First, figure out your method early on and then stick to it. Once you've committed yourself to a potty-training method (which we'll discuss in detail later on), help your child get accustomed to it by being encouraging. Second, preparedness is everything. If you're mentally and resourcefully ready, it will be less taxing on your nerves. Third, take frequent breaks and allow yourself to detach from the whole parenting process for a little while. Hang out with your friends, go watch a movie, go to a bar, and just unwind. Fourthly, make some room for error so that when accidents do happen, you get to give yourself and your child some grace. Last, if you have more than one kid, do not compare one with the other, because there's only disappointment and confusion waiting for you there.

Now that we've covered the psychological basics of potty-training let's move on to using the potty for the first time.

Chapter Five: Using the Potty for the First Time

Congratulations on making it to this part of the book. It means that you've covered almost half the book, have understood the basics, and are now ready to take their toddler on their first potty-training run. We've broken down the task into detailed, easy-to-follow steps.

1. Picking Out the Potty

This is a step we have covered, but for revision's sake, we'll touch upon it just a little. As your toddler is now ready to be potty-trained, it's recommended that you pick out the potty with them, involving them in the process by considering what they are attracted to at the store. Taking your child shopping with you will serve two purposes: It will be a nice outing and bonding time for you and your child, and it will make them feel invested in the process by having a "choice," the choice is their selection of the potty. Use phrases like "Which one do you like more?" and consider the one they point at.

If they feel inclined towards more than one, splurge a little and get them two potties. They can serve as the main potty and the backup potty back at home. In the aisle where they sell potties, there will also be peripherals such as handles, splash guards, and toys. You can buy those. And buy snacks and treats for them so the trip to buying the potty becomes associated as a rewarding trip in their minds. You can, later, use those snacks and treats as a reward for when they've gone on the potty for the first time.

2. Acquainting Them with the Potty

Now that you have shopped for the potty and have selected one suitable for your child, it's time to acquaint them with the potty at home. This differs from their picking out the potty at the store, where their curiosity and sense of wonder were piqued by the array of choices they had. Now that you have come home, that same curiosity might be replaced by them overlooking the potty. You know how kids are in terms of their attention spans.

Acquainting them with the potty at home can be done by putting the potty in the living room or their bedroom or in the toilet, and establishing to your toddler this is the new place to go potty, should they need to go.

Right now, you need not worry about getting them out of their diapers right away, as they have yet to go to on the potty for the first time. But it might be useful to notice how long they are staying dry between their peeing and pooping intervals. If they are dry for over two hours, it's time to acquaint them with the potty. Reinforce the words "poop and "pee" with the potty, so they are at least aware that that's' where they need to go. Since the potty hasn't been used yet and is clean, you can let your child play with it, sparking their sense of wonder.

3. Informing Them that Their Training has Started

Once the potty has been bought, and your child has acquainted themselves with it, it's time to have a one-on-one session with them where you tell them that their potty-training has begun. Make sure that you do not use advance or complex terms but instead use phrasing that they will be able to comprehend, such as "Now we're going to use the potty to go pee or poo, okay?" Select a phrasing and stick to it throughout the training. If you want to refer to their urine as pee and their stool as poo, that's okay. In fact, that's recommended.

For your own convenience, you can put up a chart to log in the hours they stay dry, when they went to potty, and when did they dirty their diapers, and so on. You can involve your child in this process by explaining to them what the rows and columns in the chart stand for. You can ask them if they have any questions, and then you can answer them when they ask you.

It's even better if you can watch a YouTube how-to video with them to engage them more thoroughly in the process. If your child is more of a reader, there are plenty of books on going to the potty for the first time you can read with them.

4. Having a Dry Run at the Potty

Once you and your child have communicated about the commencement of their potty-training, it's time to take them on a dry run. This is where you ask them to sit on the potty with their clothes and diapers still on. Once you have introduced them to the potty and have explained its function to them, invite them or request them politely to sit on it and don't make a grandiose thing of it right away. First, just have them sit on it ask them how it feels. They'll try to tell you what they're feeling and experiencing and will ask you question about the big hole in the middle, or the potty's handles, shape, or color. Entertain their questions with humor and tell them they have to use the potty from now on. See what their reaction is to this added information. Notice how they respond. If they respond affirmatively, it means you're good to go and can continue with the next steps of the training. If, however, they throw a tantrum or displaying negative emotions, it might be better to pause here and retry later on when they're more receptive and in the mood to interact with the potty.

5. Sticking to a Potty-Training Method

There are four main potty-training methods you can stick to. There aren't just four; it varies for each kid on a child to child basis. Let's discuss the methods.

- **Parent-led potty-training.** In this method, you, as the parent, stick to a certain schedule. One or more partners or caregivers can participate in this method, making it easier for the more people. You will allot the time for your child's toileting. The advantage of this method is that there's no need to shift your schedule massively to train your child. You can just fit everything in your timetable, provided you're consistent. The con of this method is that since you are leading the method, your child might ignore or overlook their bodily instincts altogether, relying on you to take them to the potty every time.

- **Infant potty-training.** In this potty-training method, you train your child in their infancy, i.e., one month to four months. The pro of this method is that you save a ton of money on diapers by not introducing them to your child from the start. The disadvantage is this method is very messy. In this method, you will keep an eye on your child's body signals to see when they have to go, and then you sit them down on the potty. It might require you to be intuitive, this method.

- **3-day potty-training.** We have discussed this method before in potty-training boot-camp.

- **Child-led potty-training.** In this method, you let your child adapt to the toilet on their own, not pushing or pointing them to the toilet, instead of explaining to them that when they have to go pee or poo, they should use the toilet, and then letting them adapt to it at their own pace.

This list is by no means exhaustive but covers general methods that parents use.

6. Assisting Them on their First Time

Now that we have stuck to a method, it's time to assist them on their first run at the potty. There's going to be some confusion on their end, but that's normal. First, take your child's pants off, then their diaper, and tell them to go sit on the toilet. Do this only when your intuition tells you they are about to relieve themselves. They will ask you some questions as to why they must sit on it instead of relieving themselves in their diapers. This is an excellent opportunity to explain the transition to them in terms they understand.

Once they are seated on the potty, stay with them, and tell them to let go or let loose. That they have to push to relieve themselves, this might be tricky for their first time, but if they get the hang of it, it will pay off. They might look confused, but that's natural. Tell them that there's no pressure on them, and there's no rush. If they cannot go, you can pause and repeat it later, when they are well fed and need to go.

It might do them good to distract them by way of a toy or a story since they already have a habit of going in their diapers while they are occupied with doing whatever they're doing in their regular routine. So, think of their sitting on the potty as them just sitting on a regular chair, and tell them that too in terms they will understand.

Hold their hand and gently squeeze it to set on the peristalsis that will eventually cause them to poop. Ask them if they are feeling pressure doing there, and if so, then they should relax and let it go.

This is the most critical part and should be taken as such.

7. Affirming Them after the First Time

Now that they have gone successfully their first time, it's time to reaffirm them by praising them and letting them know that they have done a good job. Give them a treat of their favorite candy or snack to let them know that they succeeded. But note that you should not make it a habit. This is for the first time only, and occasionally on every fifth or tenth successful potty session to keep them on the right track.

Explain to them that their going on the potty for the first time was an accomplishment. Kiss them, hug them, and smile at them. An excited "woohoo!" will go a long way in affirming them.

Say encouraging phrases like "You did a good job!" and "I'm so proud of you!" They won't be able to understand exactly what you're saying, but they'll pick up on the phrasing and the manner it is uttered in, thereby understanding they did something right.

8. Introducing Cleaning Methods

We are not done yet. There's still the cleaning to do. Now, since this was their first time on the potty, they cannot be expected to clean themselves on their own. You will have to assist them. Some parents decide on having their child clean themselves up right off the bat while other parents clean them up on their first few attempts. Decide on what you want to do beforehand.

If you want them to clean themselves, introduce them to toilet paper or wet wipes. For children with sensitive skin, wet wipes are a better option as they reduce the chances of rashes. For normal skin, toilet paper is how to go. For boys, teach them to wipe from back to front. For girls, it's front to back to avoid and UTIs.

If they have only peed, teach them to shake it off if they're a boy, and for girls to teach them to wipe themselves with a wipe or toilet paper.

Once they are completely clean, inform them of the importance of cleaning after going on the potty. Besides your teaching, you can play a video that explains it. There are a plethora of toddler-friendly YouTube videos that do that for you.

9. Emptying the Potty

After they have cleaned up, it's time to reinforce this part of the process but not aggressively or forcefully. It should be like presenting the casual as causal. Take the filled potty, making sure that your child is properly cleaned and is standing by as an observer, and explain to them that that contents of the potty go in the "grown-up toilet." Then, you can make it more interactive for them by having them look at the emptied contents and pushing the flush button or lever. Notice how their interest gets piqued as they see the water taking away all the contents. Ask them how that felt. Did that feel good? Do they want to do it again? If it's a hearty yes, that's good. That means they are already looking forward to the next session.

Once they have flushed, you can show them how to flush an empty toilet all over again and explaining to them the plumbing mechanics in a toddler-friendly tone. "The pipes take the poo-poo and pee-pee away."

Tell them they did a good job flushing the toilet, and that they should now move on to the next step, washing their hands.

10. Post-Potty Follow-Up

The post-potty follow up can be broken down into two steps. One: Washing their hands and explaining the importance of hygiene to them. Two: Putting their clothes back on.

The first part will be tedious for the child, as they have allotted quite a lot of time into the first potty-session, and now they are antsy to get back into their regular routine. So, you'll notice a bit of rebellion as the child tries to run away out of the bathroom. Some might be over-eager to wash their hands, mimicking the behavior they have observed in their parent. You can make things interesting for them by using a kid-friendly, bubbly soap that creates many colorful bubbles and foam. Teach them the proper way of washing their hands and drying them off with a towel.

Now you may put their clothes back on. Notice how the child feels reacquainted with a sense of normalcy once they have their clothes back on and are heading out of the bathroom, free from their training. At this time, you should not put their diaper back on. That's the next step. Just observe how your child goes about diaper-less and relieved about the house. What are they doing? Make a mental note in your head.

11. Putting their Diaper Back On

If you are following the three-day potty-training method, you might want to skip this step as this step sort of sets you back a bit in terms of the time-frame for the potty-training.

If, however, you're following the parent-led potty-training method, you should observe your kid for at least an hour and a half. During this time, if they have to go to the toilet again you should take them to the potty again. If they are dry, you should take a breather and put their diaper back on to give yourself some break and letting them reacquaint with their familiar method of relieving themselves.

Avoid pull-up pants, as they tend to halt the process of the potty-training, as we have discussed.

After you have put their diaper back on, tell your toddler why you have done so. It is for emergencies only. When they want to go again, they should tell you. Don't expect them to stick this instruction, which is why we are putting diapers on them in the first place, i.e., for room of mistakes. And considering that it was their first time on the potty, there should be a lot of room for mistakes. As with most habits, they shall perfect it the more they practice.

12. Checking the Diaper for Dryness

After putting their diaper back on, watch their behavior throughout the day—more specifically, every two hours—and check on their diaper in that time to gauge how long they stay dry. If they are keeping dry for two or over two hours, it means they are ready to continue with the routine. If, on the other hand, they aren't remaining dry for two hours, do not worry as this is just the beginning of their potty-training. In the following week they will start picking up on preferring the potty instead of their diapers, which is when we ditch the diapers altogether.

13. Asking for their Feedback

After their first potty session, ask your child how they felt, what they liked, what they disliked, what they want to do again, and if they think they are ready to keep on using the potty in place of the diaper.

Ask these questions in a way that doesn't patronize them or downplay the importance of their potty-training.

14. Sticking to a Plan

Congratulations on your first successful potty session with your toddler. This is the ripe time for making a plan and sticking to it for the next week or however long the training takes. It's critical that you stick to that plan throughout their training.

15. Repeating All of the Above

Does that sound a bit hectic? Well, it is. You have to repeat the above steps several times throughout their training. This will be a test of your patience and your resilience. It will also be an opportunity for your child to learn of the training, and that comes with its own fair share of growing pains. But since you're sticking to a plan, remaining rational throughout, and giving yourself frequent breaks, it will not be an insurmountable problem as much as it will be a manageable routine.

Chapter Six: Potty and Pooping Problems

The domain of potty training comes with its own problems. These problems can complicate the training process, making it both irritating for you as the parent and for your child as the learner. Let's discuss some major problems that might arise in training and come up with solutions for each one of them.

1. No peeing; Only Pooping

If you notice that your child is only pooping and not peeing when they use the potty, do not worry. This is only natural. In the case of some children, they develop their bowel control before they can develop their bladder control. This manifests by them only pooping and not peeing. It also manifests in the form of them wetting their diapers and the bed at night. This isn't a cause for alarm. The solution to this problem is relatively simple and does not require you to do a lot. You have only to continue with the potty-training as usual and clean the mess and swap their diapers for new ones whenever they pee involuntarily.

2. Playing with their Poop

Children are inquisitive by nature, and their inquisitive can show in them trying to play with their poop in the potty's bowl. They might try to grab it, hold it in their hand and fling it, or simply try to smell it. When that happens, you have to be stern with them, but not aggressively so. Reassert to them that poop is not meant to be played with. It's waste, it's smelly, and it dirties your hands when you touch it. Tell them that and see how they respond. If they still persist wanting to play with their poop, switch them to the adult potty with a seat so that they cannot reach their poop.

3. Your Son Sits Down to Pee

You should start training your son to stand up to pee from the start. If you notice that he wants to sit down to pee, it is a problem, but not one that cannot be tackled. Your solution to this problem should be to let your child sit down and pee at the beginning, and after they have mastered their bladder control, describe to them they have to stand up while peeing. If you're a mother trying to get him to stand up while peeing, it might be better to let their dad or one of their male caregivers to help them with the peeing process.

4. Resistance is Futile

Is your child resisting going to the potty? This might be because of a power struggle, which we have covered extensively in the previous sections. Maybe they are resisting because they are not ready yet, which is another point that we have covered thoroughly. When you see them resisting, revert to the previous step, i.e., diapers, and let them have a few days before you get back to training them. This time around, after you have communicated the importance of going to the potty, they will be less resistant and more open to the idea of using the potty.

5. Accidents

Accidents will happen. Brace yourself for that beforehand, and you will save yourself a lot of mental and physical toll. Be ready for whenever accidents happen with cleaning supplies and a fresh change of clothes. Sometimes your child might not want to go to the potty and isn't wearing a diaper either, which will result in them pooping on the floor or peeing somewhere in the living room. It is not recommended to scold or punish your child for any accidents that they cause. Punishment will make them feel ashamed and guilty and embarrassed and even rebellious.

6. Being Upset Over Flushing

Some children treat their poop and pee as part of their bodies, thinking that since they came out of their bodies, the poop and the pee are something that they should hold on to instead of flushing them, which will cause them becoming upset when you flush the toilet. It might cause them to throw a tantrum and cry, and the absolute worst-case scenario is that they will try to reach for the material being flushed. You must stop them if they try the latter. In terms of explaining to them that it is okay to flush, you can try telling them that their poop and pee are smelly and dirty and that they should be gotten rid of by flushing. If at first, they appear to be confused, that's okay. They will pick up on it in time.

7. Fear of the Toilet

While some children might be over-eager to go to the toilet, others will exhibit fear and anxiety and nervousness when using the toilet. This is exactly why we opted for a potty, as it is manageable and smaller and something that they won't be afraid of. Remember, it's a step by step process, and using the toilet comes at the end of it, not at the beginning. So, if you notice your toddler being nervous about the toilet, shift them to the potty and stick to it until you are certain that they aren't afraid anymore. It might do them good if you asked them to vocalize their fears so that you could alleviate them.

8. Wanting a Diaper When They Want to Poop

Your child is still coming to terms with using the potty, and so it is natural that they want to use a diaper when they want to poop. This will be a bit confusing for you, as you'll have already taught them to use the potty, so why do they want to go back to the diaper to poop? The answer is familiarity. They have been familiar with relieving themselves on their diapers for so long that instead of choosing the potty right away, they'll stick with the diapers. There's no cause to be frustrated at this, as with subsequent sessions, they shall start using the potty more often and grow less reliant on the diapers, and eventually will not use the diapers at all. If that sounds like a fantasy right now, trust in the training and believe that they shall outgrow their need for diapers very soon.

9. Pooping in a Specific Place Other than the Toilet

This is more of a continuation of the last point. Have you noticed that your child goes to a specific place in the house when they display signs of wanting to pee or poop? Where do they go? Do they hide behind the sofa or the curtains? Do they squat in front of the TV in the lounge and make straining faces? When you put the potty in front of them, do they resist sitting on it and instead try to revert to their previous mode of relieving? If so, there's an easy fix for that. Follow them to where they go to relieve themselves and put their potty there and ask them to go on it. Take their clothes off and put them on the potty in their familiar place and repeat that till they have become more acclimatized to the potty rather than their familiar places.

10. Bedwetting

Even though we'll cover bedwetting in the nighttime potty-training section, let's consider it for now as a potty-training problem and discuss how you can help your toddler in stopping bedwetting. Children take a long time to complete their nighttime training. More than daytime potty-training. That's because nighttime potty-training comes with its own set of challenges. The most important thing that you can do as their parent or guardian is have them go to the potty before they go to sleep, minimize the amount of liquid they consume before going to bed, and make sure that they use the potty right after they have woken up. If you want to avoid bedwetting instantly, it might be wise to use diapers for a few days until you have started their nighttime training. You can convey to them that they should inform you if they wake up during the night with the urge to go. This will require you to be on alert when they are sleeping since if they have understood what you said to them, they will come to you when they need to go, and if you're sleeping when they come to you, they'll create a mess.

11. They Only Poop or Pee Right After They've Been on the Potty

This is probably the most frustrating of the potty-training problems, and you are not to blame if you feel irritated when this happens. You sat your child down on the potty and expected them to go on it, but instead of using it, they stay dry and only go right after you pull them off the potty. They might make a mess on the floor or in their clothes. This will get jarring for you, irritating even, and you'll ask yourself why this is happening. It is happening because of pressure. They feel like they're being pressurized to perform, and being unable to do so, they make a mess. If this happens, you can either delay the potty-training until they have stopped doing this, or you can bear through the mess they make and stick to seating them down on the potty and staying with them while they try to relieve themselves.

12. They Only Go to the Potty with a Specific Person

Are there multiple caregivers at your house, besides you and your partner? Do people like your child's aunt or uncle or grandparents or a nanny? Does your child only go to the potty with a specific person? This isn't exactly a problem as much as it is a matter of your child's comfort. They are comfortable in going to the toilet with a specific person. If you want them to go to the potty with you, here are a couple of things you can try: reacquaint yourself with your toddler if for the past couple of days you feel like you have been distant with them; stay with them as they use the potty with the person they are comfortable with; and then, finally, remove the person till it's only you and the toddler on the potty.

13. Going Back to Diapers

Do you feel like your child is reverting to their diapers after having a successful run at the potty a couple of times? Try pinpointing the changes in the environment that might be causing them to revert. Are they undergoing stress? Is the potty-training routine too rigorous for them? Is there a communication gap between you and your child? Are they unable to go on the potty? Try finding the root cause of why they want to use the diapers and eliminate that cause rather than putting them back on diapers. However, if the mess-making persists, you might want to pause the potty-training right there and revert them to the diapers for the time being.

14. Hiding When They Make a Mess

Your child will hide behind furniture more often if they are making a mess somewhere in the house other than in their diapers or on the potty. Finding the mess is the easier part of this problem. You have only to follow your nose. Dealing with the child is the hard part. You will be tempted to reprimand them, but that will not be beneficial either for you or your child. You can sit them down and talk to them and try to understand what they are going through. They will try to tell you what they are feeling, and as nonsensical as their jumbled-up words sound like, it's crucial that you listen to them and try to ascertain the underlying problem. Is it confidence, or the lack of it? Is it because they have an upset stomach? Or have you possibly started the training a little too early, and they're not ready yet?

How You Can Solve Some of These Potty-Training Problems

If you are facing any of the mentioned problems—or worse, many of them at the same time—it is only natural that you have felt frustrated with the lack of progress in your training. Let's go over some methods you can apply in your training to make things easier for you and your toddler.

Reverse Psychology

More specifically: Pretending like you do not care. Does this sound a little too cold? Well, it need not be. You are not expected to become so aloof that your child starts craving for your attention. But you have to pretend like you're not too frustrated by the hitch in their training. It will take some of the pressure off your child and let them get reacquainted with their routine. Once they are back in their comfort zone, they will start to take potty-training a bit more candidly. Why does reverse psychology work? It's because some children have a knack for saying no to whatever you propose to them. It's not something they do on purpose; rather, it's an essential part of their growing up. It has nothing to do with how you have been training them so far. It's just that they have learned an unfamiliar word, i.e., "no," and are just now getting to understand its connotations.

An example of reverse psychology would be you telling them that if they haven't gone to the potty yet, it's completely okay. This way, you will not have to take them to the park and can stay home all day. Now, in this scenario, if your child really loves going to the park, they'll start thinking, "Oh no, I really wanted to go to the park, and now we're not going." After doing this once or twice, notice how they go to the potty on their own. Potty-training reverse psychology is an excellent tool to have at your disposal. If it makes you feel a bit evil, well, don't. You're dealing with a toddler here, and excluding punishment and reprimanding, everything goes here.

Cutting Back on Their Rewards

If you started giving your child rewards every time they used the potty, there's a good chance that you have done something Pavlovian. They now associate going to the potty with the reward they will get, and whenever you do not offer them a reward, they'll get antsy and irritated and will be unable to use the potty.

If this is the case, consider scaling back on their rewards and getting back into the training without a lot of hurrah and here-you-go involved. Consider this: They aren't always going to get a reward every time they go use the potty. Are you possibly spoiling them with way too many rewards? This might be unintentional, as giving them the promise of rewards if they successfully go to the potty can be an appealing, easy fix for a problem that seems to have no solution at the moment.

By cutting down on their rewards and reasserting that they have to go on the potty, you'll be better able to deal with their Pavlovian desire to have a treat every time they use the potty.

This also holds true for stars and colors that go on their potty-training chart. At some point, you have to scale back on the celebratory nature of their potty usage. It's better if it's sooner than later.

Fixing Their Constipation Issues

Sometimes it's not because of your child's moods they aren't able to use the potty as much as it is about their physical incapability to use it. Case in point—constipation. Notice if the child is crankier than usual and is always on edge whenever it's potty time. Are they grunting and straining more than usual? If so, it might be that they are constipated. Introduce high-fiber foods in their diets, such as green vegetables and whole-grain bread, to help them with their constipation. Be careful, though, as introducing more than the recommended dose of high-fiber foods in their diet will have a negative effect on their stomach's health.

Is Your Child Testing You?

A child's cognitive growth allows them to understand your patterns and test the limits you have imposed on them. This might come off as rebellion to us grownups, but for a child, these little acts of rebellions ("No" in response to a request you made, throwing tantrums when you try to force them to do something, and throwing stuff around the house in anger) make perfect sense. But you aren't expected to stand by idly either. Be firm about the limits that you have set up and stick to them, regardless of their throwing a tantrum or straight-up refusing.

You're the adult here, not them. You know what's better for your child, not them. Here, again, reverse psychology can come into play and make them think that they've got control instead of you. Once that has been asserted, they'll want to go to the toilet on their own. Whether or not they are testing you or not, the fact remains that sooner or later, they have to use the potty.

Chapter Seven: Nighttime Potty Training

Nighttime potty-training is in a whole different ballpark of its own, requiring a separate, detailed chapter where we will cover the basics, some tips, and the time it shall take your toddler to be trained. Let's get right into it.

Difference Between Daytime and Nighttime Potty-Training

There are several differences between daytime and nighttime potty-training, the most marked one being their different bowel and bladder movements. Of course, your child has by now gotten a little control over their bladder and bowels. You can observe this by their daytime potty-training habits, but what about nighttime? Well, nighttime training requires them to have more control over these two muscles than daytime because they lose voluntary control while they are sleeping. You might notice this in the form of bedwetting and even pooping while they are asleep. This is no cause for alarm or worry. This is exactly why we are covering nighttime training. A potty-training expert, Samantha Allen, says that potty-training is a daytime process and that you cannot be expected to teach someone something when they have lost consciousness, i.e., when they are sleeping. You can, however, she adds, set your kid up to successfully stay dry during the night.

Remember that nighttime training requires a lot of developmental prerequisites, the most important one being control over their muscles. Subconscious control. Your child might be excelling at their daytime potty-training, but they'll be able only to successfully train for nighttime when they have covered a few developmental milestones. Another important milestone that they need to cover is their eating and drinking habits. Last, it's the hormone that suppresses urine production at night that is the most crucial factor in their nighttime training. If the production of that hormone has not started yet, their training cannot be complete. If you try to persevere through that phase—without the assistance of the hormone—you are going to impact the child's self-esteem and confidence, making them confused and irritated. It will make them dread going to the toilet.

Nighttime potty-training happens way later than daytime potty-training. Unless your child has mastered all elements of daytime potty-training, they cannot be expected to excel in nighttime potty-training.

When to Start Nighttime Potty-Training

Consider nighttime potty-training once your child displays signs of readiness. Some signs of readiness to look out for include:

1. Seeing that their diaper is warm when they wake up. If it is cold, they are not ready for nighttime potty-training. The warm diaper signifies that your child is wetting their diaper after they have woken up. A cold diaper suggests that they went sometime during the night when they were asleep. Additionally, notice if their diaper has poop in it when they wake up. Normally it should not have poop in it, but if there are signs, it might be better to hold off the training till their diapers are void of poop. Remember, this is not the child's fault since

their bodies are undergoing involuntary, unconscious motions when they are asleep.

2. Once you have ascertained that their diapers are warm and wet instead of cold and wet, the next sign to look out for readiness is checking to see how frequently their diapers are dry when they wake up in the morning. If their diapers are frequently dry, it means that they have started getting control of their bladder while they are asleep. This might be because of the hormone production or because their bladder has strengthened. In both cases, it is a major win.

3. The last step to look out for in terms of readiness is your child asking that you remove their diaper or nappies when they want to sleep. This signifies that they are confident that they won't wet the bed while asleep. This also signifies their want for independency. Again, in both cases, this is a major win as you have progressed beyond all three signs and are now ready to teach your toddler nighttime training.

If you want further clarification in terms of whether they are ready or not, ask yourself these questions: Is your child able to follow simple directives? Are they physically able to go to the bathroom? Can they get on the potty or the toilet on their own? Are they staying dry for longer than two hours? If the answer to most of those questions is yes, your child is ready for nighttime potty-training. If all the signs of readiness are there, it's better that you start their nighttime training sooner than later since if you delay the process, it might cause complications with their daytime training. The typical age for nighttime training is between 2 years to 3 years. Ideally, if the child has gone a few weeks with no incidents, it's best to commence their training.

How Long Does Nighttime Potty-Training Last?

It's only natural to wonder how long this training shall last, as you'll already have mastered daytime training by now. Well, most children can get through an entire night by the age of four to five. Bedwetting, however, is going to persist a little longer till after they are five since it is a developmental deficiency rather than one concerned with chronological age. If you have a daughter, you will notice that there's going to be a slight difference between training her and training a son. It isn't that big of a difference, but for clarification's sake, we shall cover it at length in the next chapter.

You can expect nighttime training to last for around one to two months, as there's going to be a lot of nights where inconsistencies occur, some nights where they wet the bed, some weeks where they won't even get it once. It's a lot to take in, which is why we have prepared some tips that you can follow to make sure everything goes smoothly. Again, here patience is the biggest virtue that will see you through this part of their training. Patience and empathy. Understand that nighttime training is relatively harder than daytime training and that your toddler is doing all they can to learn the ropes.

Tips You Can Follow

If you want to ditch the overnight diapers, follow these tips to make sure that your child is getting the most out of their nighttime training.

1. Setting Up a Consistent Daytime Training Plan

The success of nighttime training depends upon the consistency of daytime training. Both of them are directly proportional. Once it has been a few weeks—or better yet, a month and a half—you can start their nighttime training. The potty-training plan for their daytime training must be individualized to suit your child. It's not a one-schedule-fits-all kind of deal.

Let's go over the basics of daytime potty-training: They stay dry for two or more hours, they have started using the potty on their own, they can pull off their clothes and put them on once they are done, and they can wash their hands.

Now consider how that affects their nighttime training. Once you have started, let them know that they should go to the potty once before they are going to sleep, and once during the middle of the night when they wake up. You can communicate this with them in easy-to-follow, simple directives that do not boggle or confound them. Don't expect them to follow these steps right off the bat. It will take some time. Meanwhile, keep on training them in daytime training irrespective of the progress of their nighttime training. Their confidence in their daytime training will play a key role in their nighttime training.

2. Taking Your Family History

If your parents are available to talk to, you should ask them how long it took you to potty-train both in the daytime and in the nighttime. Ask them about the methods they used to train you, what worked for them and what didn't work for them. Ask them about the age that you stopped wetting the bed, the age at which you went to the potty without their assistance, and the age at which you ditched your diapers. It shall be a little nostalgic walk down the memory lane, and an excellent opportunity for you to learn about your history. Later, you can use that knowledge to your advantage by implementing it in your child's life

Kids take after their parents, and not just in matters of their appearance. They emulate the same habits, the same taste in things, and the same dislikes. Knowing about yourself will give you an insight into the behavior of your toddler in an altogether new way. This isn't limited to just you. Encourage your partner to ask their parents about their history. To expand the information pool, you can ask your uncles and aunts about their experiences with your cousins.

Accidents such as bedwetting run in the family. Knowing whether or not you used to wet the bed will inform you about the child's tendencies.

3. Limiting their Liquid Intake

To prevent nighttime bedwetting, the most recommended route is limiting your child's liquid intake after the evening. Ideally, you should not let them drink anything after dinner. But this is not a hard and fast rule, as your child is bound to feel thirsty sometime after dinner. The easy fix to that is getting one of those brightly colored plastic shot glasses. Filling them with water or milk or juice will not only quench your child's thirst, but it shall make them feel like they have drunk a substantial amount of liquid because they will see the glass as full and not its small size.

Sugary liquids are a hard no after dinner, as these tend to fill up the bladder with more water as compared to plain water.

In any case, you should not introduce your child to soft drinks that early on. It's not good for their teeth – as well as their health. If your child is lactose intolerant, they're bound to make a mess in bed if you feed them milk. The water that you give them at dinner and after dinner should not be too cold, as chilly water also induces the need to urinate.

4. Make Them Use the Potty Before They Go to Bed and After They Wake Up

Once you have decided on potty-training your child in the nighttime, you must have them go to the potty at least once before they go to bed. Ideally, you should have them go on the potty half an hour before bedtime. On a tangential note, this is an excellent opportunity to form the habit of nighttime brushing. But since it's just their milk teeth, it's okay if they don't pick the habit of nighttime brushing right away. You can be lenient in that regard.

Take them to the potty first thing after they have woken up and have them sit on it for a few minutes to empty their bladder and bowel. Again, this is an excellent time to get them in the habit of brushing their teeth after waking up. The sooner they pick up on that habit, the better.

Notice the consistency of their potty routine before and after they wake up. If they are sticking to it regularly, it means that their nighttime potty-training is progressing at a good pace. Now might be the time to pat yourself on the back for a job well done, but not too hard a pat, as we're not out of the training routine yet.

5. Preparing for Potential Accidents

Nighttime potty-training accidents are considerably different from daytime ones, the most prominent and irritating problem—both for you and your toddler—being bedwetting. In this case, you should prepare by double layering the sheets, using a plastic sheet under those sheets to make sure that the wetness doesn't soak up in the mattress, and keeping a spare change of clothes, diapers, and sheets at hand should they wet the bed. A very thorough method to counter bedwetting includes adding a waterproof protector, a sheet on top of that, then another layer of waterproof protector, and last, another sheet on top of that. When they do wet the bed, you can strip off the two layers on top and not have to worry about changing the two sheets below. If you're looking for a quick fix, consider adding pee pads under the sheets.

6. Should You Wake Them Up in the Night, or Not?

This is the big one. Should you or shouldn't you wake them up during the night? Some parents who are rigorous about the nighttime training wake up their child whether or not their child is a deep sleeper. That is not recommended, as by waking up the child who's a light sleeper, you'll disturb the rest of their sleep cycle, thereby making them irritated and vexed unnecessarily. Only wake your child up in the night if you're certain that they can fall asleep easily once they're done using the potty. However, if it feels exhausting after the first few attempts, you can skip this part of the training and move on to the next one, as this isn't as crucial to their nighttime training as the other steps.

7. Checking their Dryness Patterns

Keep a vigilant check on how long they stay dry for after they have woken up, and if their diapers are dry at all right after they wake up. If their diapers are remaining dry for a week, it's time to skip them altogether and try making them sleep without diapers or pull-up pants.

8. Following their Lead

In the case of one parent, their five-year-old son started telling them that he was ready for nighttime training. The parent did not ask their son, nor did they push him in any way. The child-initiated the nighttime training because he wanted to be dry in his bed.

Take note from that example and try to follow your child's lead. They're in tune with their body, as much as a child can be, and sometimes they know better when to start. Do not force them or try to get them jump-started as this will—as we have mentioned numerous times—aggravate the problem instead of solving it.

9. Celebrating the Little Things

Once they have progressed to keeping the bed and their diapers dry for a week or so, celebrate this milestone with them by giving them their favorite treat, watching a movie with them, or taking them toy shopping.

10. Understanding the Cause

There might be an underlying cause to their bedwetting. It can be a health issue. If you notice them consistently wetting the bed, take them to a pediatrician and discuss what the problem might be. It might be uneven hormone production or a weak bladder. In either case, the doctor shall prescribe you medication and a dietary regimen to follow.

Chapter Eight: Potty Training Girls vs. Boys

Potty-training, a girl, differs from training a boy. Regardless, it's a challenge in both cases. Let's look at the distinct differences between training a girl and a boy.

Boys Take a Little Longer to Train

Boys do not show interest in using the potty in the beginning. Girls, in comparison, are more receptive to it. Because of that, boys are slower to master potty-training. The myth that boys are longer to train than girls originates from here. This isn't exactly true. The time frame for both their training is almost the same. It's just that boys start a little later. In terms of completing the training, the approximate time stays the same regardless of their gender. In a poll of 1300 moms that was conducted by Made for Moms, it was found that roughly 56 percent of girls were potty-trained by the age of 2-1/2 months, while only 44 percent of boys were trained by that age. While this isn't exactly a big difference, if you are a diaper-buying parent, this small difference can seem longer in terms of the economics of it all.

Boys Have to Learn Two Different Ways of Going

Boys have to learn how to stand up to pee and then sit down to poop while girls only have to learn how to sit down. Some parents teach their boys to stand up first and then sit on the potty later. Other parents do the opposite; they teach their sons to sit down and do both poop and pee on the potty and then teach them how to stand up and pee. The tricky part is teaching them to aim their pee in the toilet such that it does not cause splashes. If you are teaching them to pee while standing up, only move on to them sitting down once they have mastered peeing standing up, and where you are teaching them to sit down, only move on to standing up once they have mastered sitting down. Of course, the rules with pooping are different. The previous instructions are for peeing only. When it comes to pooping, both boys and girls have the same method, i.e., sitting down. They may even pee during their pooping session, which is only natural and should be encouraged.

Girls Mature Faster than Boys

This isn't a myth. Girls, indeed, develop faster than boys in terms of intelligence and physiology. Girls also develop language skills faster than boys, which allows them to understand your instructions quicker, thus making it easier to potty-train them. Girls also learn how to take their dresses off and put them on faster than boys, and gain control of their bladder and bowel faster than boys, all of which makes it easier to train them. But note that the period for the training remains the same for both boys and girls.

Now let's make a side-by-side comparison for boys and girls in various stages of their potty-training.

Potty-Training Commencement Based on their Gender

Although the *when* of it all depends upon the individual child more than any pre-existing guideline, the gender of the child can play a huge role in deciding when to start their training.

Boys: Boys will take their time in being developmentally ready to start potty-training. Thus, their training will be delayed as compared to girls. How delayed, you ask? Well, a few months give or take. The factors that decide on their readiness include their interest in potty-training, the development of their bowel and bladder control, and their routine. Most parents who are training their boys say that they start teaching them at the age of two.

Girls: Girls are quicker to adapt to potty-training early on. They will manifest this by showing interest in going to the potty. If you have a girl, you can start training her at the age of 18 months. Before that, they will not be completely ready.

While these are the approximate times to start their training, remember that for each child, the case is different, regardless of their gender, where some are early adopters, other moderate learners, and some slow to learning potty-training. To see if they are ready for potty-training, consult the first chapter in the book to see the signs of their readiness.

One other difference in choosing when to start potty-training the child is their choice of distraction. Girls tend to be more on the reserved side in most cases, relying on subtler toys and music and movies to distract themselves. In contrast, boys are a little rowdier, relying on louder toys, louder videos, and videogames to keep themselves occupied. This is yet another reason why girls pick up on potty-training than boys, as they aren't as distracted with their playtime as boys are. Boys are more preoccupied with their toys and games and movies, and so can be tricky when teaching them how to use the potty.

Adjusting Potty-Training Techniques for the Child Based on their Gender

If you are a parent to more than one child, you may have seen that your older child was quite different to train than your younger one. If the older child was a girl, then she might have taken less time to train. If it was a boy, he might have taken more time to train. You have to remember to change and try different techniques for potty-training, and sometimes, you must come up with a customized technique you haven't used before.

Boys: Boys will sit on the potty, go, and then get up and say that they are finished. They won't be concerned with cleaning themselves up right away. Also, when it comes to wiping, for boys, this is not a big concern, as they can both wipe back to front and front to back.

Girls: But girls must wipe front to back, or else they will contract bacterial infections in their vagina. Girls will also be quicker to adapt to the potty as they'll want to be a "big girl" badly.

Ten Gender-Specific Tips to Help Your Toddler

Tip #1

Girls: Choosing Size-Appropriate Seats

Buying a potty that's smaller and compact is recommended for your girl. This will reduce the chances of splashing while peeing, and the chances of them falling inside it. Boys tend to need bigger potties than girls. For us, our adult-sized toilet might seem very normal and manageable in size but think of it from your daughter's perspective. It's a goliath porcelain throne!

Boys: Getting the Green Light

If you start training your boy before you have their consent, it's going to backfire on you. First, make sure that they're ready, and then start their training. This way, they will throw no tantrums or grow fussy about going to the potty. They have to be interested, they have to be willing to try it, and they must be physically capable of going to the potty before their training can begin.

Tip #2

Girls: They Wanna Have Fun

Talking to your girl in a candid, friendly, and exciting manner about their toilet training, and explaining every step in an affirming manner will go a long way in them being receptive to their training. Make it fun, make it exciting; make it memorable.

Boys: Squatting First, Standing Second

It's not etched in stone or anything, but it's better if you teach your boy to sit down first to pee and poop, and then learn how to stand up and pee later.

Tip #3

Girls: Looking Cute Will Get You Results

Girls are extremely interested in buying colorful underwear for themselves. Use that as an incentive to train them by taking them out underwear shopping. Pick out the ones they like the most, and make them wear them when they're at home. Who doesn't like buying fresh, new, exciting underwear?

6. Boys: Let Them be Pants-Free

There's no shame in letting your boy roam around the house, not wearing any pants. If they're doing that of their own volition, let them. If you want to quicken the process, do it yourself. Take off their pants and their diapers and just leave them with their shirt on. When they have to go, they'll let you know, and you can take them to the potty. If they make a mess, at least they won't dirty their pants or use any diapers. So, win/win situation, right?

Tip #4

Girls: Treating Them to Some Sweets

Girls will be more receptive to sweet treats than boys because boys are more likely to be immersed in some activity while going on their potty as compared to girls. So, what incentive should girls be offered in place of immersion? The answer is simple. Sweets. Mini M&Ms are the best sort of treats to give them after every successful potty run. You can give them one for when they go number one, two for when they go number two, and three if they wipe properly. Think of it as sweetening the deal for them. Do you remember that your parents used to give you treats when you went to the potty as a child? If you do, think of the positive effect this will have on her long-term memory when she recalls this as an adult.

Boys: They Want to Have Some Fun as Well

For boys, the entire process of potty-training should be a fun-centric one, as it appeals to their nature. For girls, this isn't as big of an issue. But for boys, you will have to make sure that their peripheral interest is captivated by the book, a song, a movie on their tablet, or a toy that they like. At first, it shall be just a source of distraction, but down the road, it will become a sort of a stimulus to go and use the potty more often. And that's what we want, right?

Tip #5

Girls: The Importance of Wiping

As we have discussed before, this is not a problem for boys as much as it is for girls. Boys can wipe either way, and that's fine, as long as they're cleaning themselves up properly. For girls, you must teach them the correct way to wipe. Do you remember what that is from the previous sections of the book? That's right: from the front to the back; this is crucial to feminine health! Girls have an opening to their most precious organs, and if teach them to wipe back to front, they will be bringing up germs and bacteria to that opening, causing urinary tract infections, which can be both very painful are very irritating. They're hell to get rid of, considering the age of the child.

Boys: Focusing on Getting it Done

For boys, try to get their potty-training done as quickly as possible once you have begun. This is because dragging it on for weeks or even months will not help them or you. Your boy will lose interest if the process takes too long, showing this by way of throwing a tantrum or getting irritated when they have to go to the bathroom. Besides, think of it from your perspective: you will get sidetracked by all the things going in your own life. This will eventually lead to frustration on both ends, and we don't want that. Just stay consistent, wrap it up as conveniently and quickly as you can, and you'll see the benefits of it in both your lives.

Tip #6

Girls: What Does Going to the Bathroom Entail?

Kids, and specifically girls, are very literal in terms of interpreting your commands. When you tell your girl to go to the bathroom, what exactly does she understand from that phrase? Does it mean that she'll go inside the bathroom and come out without doing anything? Of course not, but she may not understand that. You have to give her step-by-step instructions to go to the bathroom, use the potty, and then wash her hands. Trust her in that she'll understand it as long as you have explained it very simply and clearly.

Boys: Make Them Comfortable First

Comfort is a big issue for boys, as unlike girls, they have dangly bits in terms of private parts. The diaper or the underwear might be causing them suffocation down there, what with everything packed so tightly that it debilitates their movement. If you notice that that's the case, buy them new underwear and choose diapers that are a size larger.

Another way you can make things comfortable for him is by checking to see if he's using the potty easily. Some potties, although they're generically the ideal size for your child, do not sit well with your son. He might want a bigger or a comfier potty, preferably with a bigger bowl and handles. If they're feeling uncomfortable still, it might be better to skip the potty altogether and put them on the grown-up toilet with a child seat on top.

Tip #7

Girls: Do-It-Yourself Toilets

Girls by their nature, want things to be clean, tidy, sparkly, and, well, how do I put it, girly. A do-it-yourself potty is a perfect opportunity to get their interest aroused in potty-training. Take her shopping with you and buy a DIY potty kit that she likes. Take it home with her and help her assemble it, put glitters and stickers on it, and let her become familiar with it. If she treats it like she treats her doll-house or dolls, she will become devoted to it and spend more time on it. It's simple child psychology at play here.

Boy: Don't Make Them Bored

Today's parents notice an interesting difference between boys and girls, often stating that boys are more likely to want to have fun, and girls want to be cleaner – in general. This translates to potty-training, as well. Your boy is easily distracted by distractions in their immediate environment, such as their videogames, toys, books, etc. If they get bored by sitting on the potty, they're not going to want to repeat the dreadful ritual. Instill their interest by adding their favorite games into the mix, so the potty-training time is associated with fun and excitement rather than boredom. Boys aren't as concerned with making a mess as girls are. Boys will look at it as a matter-of-fact thing they did and move on. Girls are likelier not to want to make a mess.

Tip #8

Girls: Let Them Know You're Proud

Letting your baby girl know that mama and dada are proud of her for going to the bathroom is not only going to serve as a well-needed ego boost for her self-esteem but remind her that she's doing something right. What's that, you ask? That's her going to the bathroom successfully. By giving your girl her love and adoration, you'll be setting her up to go to the bathroom more favorably than before, since she wants to become a grownup fast. This is because of the physiological and mental development difference between boys and girls, making girls mature faster, and thus wanting to appear older faster than boys.

16. Boys: An Alarm Clock Will Do Wonders

And we don't mean an actual alarm clock. It's you who must turn into their alarm clock, alerting them that they have to go to the bathroom. That's because boys are more energetic by nature, and they constantly run around, playing, screaming, experimenting, interacting, and experiencing new things all the time. In this time, if they have a diaper on them, they'll go in it, and boom, back to playing. But if they don't have a diaper on, they'll make a mess, and we don't want that. So, pick a duration of time beforehand, and remind your son to go to the bathroom at each interval, telling them they can play later once they're done with their pooping and peeing. We'll discuss this in more detail in the next chapter, i.e., Forming Potty Habits.

Tip #9

Girls: Ditching their Diapers

By their nature. girls want to appear older than they are when they're little. Call it the big girl effect, call it mimicking, whatever suits you - it's a fact! There's a reason the colloquialism "boys will be boys" is so popular; it's because boys are prone to staying juvenile longer than girls. So, when it comes to ditching diapers, it will be different for your girl. Here you have swap her diapers for underwear altogether, stressing that now they are a big girl and that diapers are for little girls. Their minds will be able to comprehend and implement it faster than you think.

Boys: Introduce a Little Competition in the Mix

Boys are competitive by nature. Use this to your advantage. Add competition to the mix by giving them something to aim at the toilet. While we previously discussed dyes and Cheetos, try to add something a little different. Maybe colorful biodegradable rings that are easy to flush? How about cereal? Tell them to aim their pee at the cereal and hit every single one of them. When they feel that they're pitted in a battle of wits against cereal, they'll make sure to come out on the other side, victorious.

Tip #10

Girls: Acquaint Them with Your Potty-Time

Although your little girl is growing up quickly and adapting to everything that you're teaching her, it might do her training well if you helped her by way of showing instead of telling. Hey, it works in writing fiction, it can very well translate to potty-training and work here too. You can take them to the bathroom with you and demonstrate the way that you go about going number one, going number two, and how you wipe yourself. Also, when your daughter sees that other members of the family are also using the toilet, it will automatically click in her head that it's something grown-ups do, and her desire to become a grown-up herself will catalyze the training process.

Boys: Time for their Big-Boy Underwear

As we previously discussed, getting big-girl underpants for your girl is going to have an enormous impact on how she sees potty-training. Well, it holds true for boys. Time to take them out on a trip to their favorite clothing store and to pick out some underpants that they like. Normally, the selection will include action heroes, trains, or something that they are specifically interested in, so let their imaginations run wild; let them choose the ones they want. Be aware beforehand, they are going to favor the superhero underpants! It might be Batman's logo that they want to cover their tooshie or Spiderman's webbed underwear. You can help them pick out several underwear that will make them excited for their training, as they'll get to see their underwear more and more whenever they take their clothes off and when they are sitting on the potty. Makes sense, right?

Chapter Nine: Forming Potty Habits

Potty-training isn't just a discrete task. It comes with peripheral habits that are necessary to teach your toddler. Some of these essential potty habits include:

Managing Paper-Waste

Toilet paper waste management should be taught to the toddler from day one. Whether it's them who's doing the wiping or you are doing it for them, teach them that the toilet paper is *not* something that you should throw away in the trash bin. Rather, it's something that should be flushed away. Make them understand that it's smelly, that it's bad, that it must not be touched from the dirty end, that it should be gotten rid of right after they or you are done using it, *and that the only proper way to get rid of it is by flushing it.* After showing them how to flush it once or twice, you should let them throw it in the toilet and flush it themselves to form the habit.

Flushing

Whether you're teaching them how to flush their used toilet paper or the contents of their potty, getting your child to flush the toilet is another important habit that should be taught early on. If your toilet has a lever, you can make a fun game out of it called "pull the lever." If it's a button, it can get a little tricky, as most buttons are a little harder to push for toddlers. If that's the case, then you should assist them by pressing the button with them. If that's impossible, at least have them accompany you when you flush the toilet, so they know that that's part of the potty process.

Washing Up

Okay, so washing their hands is another essential part of their potty-training and a very vital habit of picking up on early on. Right after they've gone potty their first time, you should introduce them to the concept of soaping their hands up, turning the tap on, lathering, rinsing, and cleaning their hands under the flow of water, turning the tap off, and drying their hands on a towel. Sometimes, children get scared of all the routine. In that case, break it down into a series of steps that you can teach them one by one. First, just have them become familiarized with the sink. You can put up a stool in front of the sink - and should have a kiddie stool that is both colorful and sturdy. Distract them by showing them their reflection on the mirror above the sink. Then acquaint them with the faucet. There are a variety of children-friendly soaps available in the market, soaps that make a lot of bubbles, soaps that are very fragrant, and soaps that are very colorful. Pick any of those to make the washing up routine more cheerful and playful for them. You can add a variety of toddler-friendly towels too.

Taking Aim

Girls won't have this issue as they'll have to pee sitting down. Boys must be taught how to pee standing up. This is a habit that will form over a week or a couple of weeks. It will create a mess for the first few days, during which they won't be able to control their stream. You can teach them to hold their penis and direct their stream at the water in the bowl. If they're not getting the hang of it (pun intended), you can train them to sit down and pee for the first few days and try again once they're comfortable with peeing while sitting.

Emptying the Toilet

After they are finished using the potty, tell them that their waste needs to go in the toilet and needs to be flushed. For the first few weeks, you'll likely be doing this yourself. But after the second or third week, they should be able to empty the potty on their own and be able to flush the contents. However, this is a very temporary habit, as they won't always be using the potty. In the next chapter, we shall be covering the transition from potty to the adult toilet. If this feels too tedious of a habit for your toddler, you can skip it.

Putting Their Clothes Back On

With boys, they might want to roam around naked in the house. This might be fine for a few days, but this cannot go on forever, can it? They need to be taught how to put their clothes back on. Are they able to pull their clothes off before going on the potty? If they're able to do that, then they're also able to put their clothes back on after they're done. You're going to have to assist them for a week for that before they're able to do that one their own.

Informing a Parent/Caregiver They Have to Go

Before they're completely independent, your child has to inform an adult they need to go. Cultivate this habit early in their training to avoid messes. If you're available, they should be able to tell you they have to go. If a caregiver such as a nanny or a grandparent is available, they should be able to tell them that. The easiest way to get them to do that is by being frank and candid with the child. The child will only confide in the person they are comfortable with. They'll turn away from the person who scolds and reprimands them. And we've already covered how punishments and scolding are very counterintuitive and have no place in potty-training.

The average time it takes for a person to form a habit is 21 days. Do you want to form your child's potty-going habit? Why not try the 21-day technique? It's neither too long nor too short. Just 21 days sounds manageable, right?

Let's break the process down into a 21-day plan that you can easily follow. We'll cover the first eight days of the 21 days. You can repeat the routine described below for the rest of the 13 days.

1. This is the most important day for their potty-training. Choose Saturday as the starting point so that you're not busy, and so you have the whole weekend ahead to give all your attention to the habit-forming routine. On this day, wake up as early as you can and wake up your toddler half an hour after you have woken up. The half-hour window is for you to get ready, go to the bathroom, get some breakfast. Once you've done all that, wake your toddler up and check his or her diaper. What do you see? Is it just pee, or is there poop inside it too? If there's poop too, it might not be the right time to get them off diapers. Consider that for later in the routine. If it's just pee, is the pee warm or cold? If it's cold, it means that they recently wet it in their sleep. If it's warm, or better yet, dry, it means that they can stay dry for longer than two hours in their sleep. This is good; this is progress.

Now take your child to the potty and have them go at it. If they go naturally, that's good. If they don't, consider putting them on the potty later in the day; once they are done, put their diaper back on. Throughout the rest of the day, you have to keep checking their diaper at every two-hour interval to see if they're staying dry or not. Half the training comprises of getting them out of their diapers. So, the first 11 days of the training will be concerned with weaning them off of diapers. How is your child responding to their first day of potty-training? If they're responding well, it's a good sign, and it bodes well for the rest of the 20 days. In the evening, after dinner, limit their liquid intake and see how they respond to that. Take them to the potty about every two hours. If you haven't started a chart for yourself, make one. These days there are a ton of apps that come with pre-made charts for your potty-training routine, so take advantage of the easiest app you can find. It's even better than written charts because that way, you get reminders in the form of chimes and alerts on your phone. At the end of the day, have them go to the potty one last time, then put their diaper on, and tuck them in their bed.

2. The second day, Sunday will involve you doing the same things as Saturday, except now might be a time to have a one-on-one talk with your toddler about their training. Using simple, toddler-comprehendible terms, tell them about what you two did yesterday and how that's important and should be continued for the next 19, 20 days. Make them aware of their potty-training.

You can reward them for understanding this. Now, again with the two-hour intervals, keep a check on their diaper dryness.

3. Make sure you're sticking to the routine by constantly checking the charts and assist them if they need assistance in going to the potty. You can ease them in by playing with them, keeping them occupied, and rewarding them every second or third attempt on the potty. Try to keep an eye out for them pooping or peeing elsewhere if they are avoiding the potty. Repeat the nighttime routine by tucking them in the bed after making them use the potty and putting a fresh diaper on them.

4. Now, this is a tricky day, as it's a Monday, the most dreaded of all days. If you're a parent with a job, it means you have to leave your baby with a caregiver or a daycare. Before, daycares often try to hasten the process of potty-training, thereby botching it and causing emotional and mental scarring to the child. If you can find a suitable daycare that guarantees that they don't rush the process, that's better. But you should confirm it by observing them potty-train your child once or twice, just to be sure. You can ask your toddler about the potty-training at daycare once they're home with you. If their expressions and words suggest confusion and fear, the daycare is doing them more harm than good.

Caregivers, on the other hand, include nannies and relatives such as grannies, are an excellent resource because they have trained other kids before, and they're going to give your kid the personal attention they need. Before you head into work, take note of your child's diaper's dryness and wetness and jot it down in your chart. Keeping note of everything is key here. That's why we recommended getting an app in the beginning. If you're more of a journaling person, always keep a diary at hand . It's for your convenience, as it will point out a pattern to you after the first week has passed, the pattern being of their toileting times, their consistency, the nature of their stool and pee, and when they wet their diapers during sleep and when they stay dry.

5. Day four gets a little easier as you move on to Tuesday. Repeat the same routine as before, being mindful of the charts, being aware of your child's behavior, and discussing their potty-training with the daycare or the caregiver. If you're on the job, notice that your lack of presence affects the child differently. Supplement for the time lost by playing with them, attending them when they call for you, and being a bit more immersed in their potty-training routine during the hours you're home.

6. You are in the middle of the week, the worst two days have come and gone, and now you can relax a bit and notice how your relaxation is emulated in your child. It's likely (and at least hopeful) that they have picked on their training, they are more receptive to it, and they are inclined on their own to use the potty. But you should not ditch their diapers just yet. For that, we must arrive at day seven.

7. On Thursday, take your toddler out and splurge on some underwear that they like. Pick out at least three to four of them so that you have an easy time cleaning them when or if they make a mess in them. These underwear are for their diaper ditching process. Once back home, carry on with the two-hour routine as usual. You'll start noticing that their diapers stay dry for longer than two hours now. This is because they are adapting to the training. Please note that if at any step of the training you feel like they are regressing, stop the training for a few days. If the progress is uniform and consistent, keep on keeping on. If you were offering rewards every day to your child for successful potty-runs, consider dialing them back down, as too many rewards tend to spoil your child and create a Pavlovian effect.

8. TGIF! It's likely that you don't have to work tomorrow (and you deserve that break!) You've got the entire weekend to yourself and your child, and you can devote this time to the next step of your potty-training, i.e., diaper ditching. Goodbye, diapers, we do not need for you anymore. Today you should closely observe your child's diapers - more rigorously than any other preceding day. If things go as planned, they are close to not needing them any longer.

If they're keeping dry for over three hours, it's time to save a ton of money on diapers. Replace those diapers with the underwear you bought!

Notice how excited your child gets when they wear their new underwear and notice how eagerly they use the potty. Since now they're not going to be wearing diapers at night, you should be more vigilant about their nighttime liquid consumption and taking them to the potty before they sleep.

Expect accidents to happen. Prepare for them by wet-proofing their bed, as discussed in the nighttime training section.

9. We're back on Saturday. You can relax into your weekend routine by waking up at a normal time, treating yourself to some breakfast, and enjoying a well-deserved break from your parenting for about a good half-hour. Often, we, as the parents, forget to take care of ourselves while we're focusing on our child. Our self-care is equally important. Go check your child's bed. If the bed is dry and if they're sleeping soundly, you can let them sleep a little longer and maybe catch up with some friends on the phone, read a book, watch something on Netflix, or hang out with your partner. Are there any chores around the house that need doing that are impossible to get done with your baby around? Make use of this time and some chores.

Wake your toddler up later than usual, take them to the bathroom and have them use the potty. Remember that they're not always going to poop or pee in the potty, but you still have to take them so the habit forms and becomes concrete.

Since today is their first day without diapers, observe their behavior as they go about their day. What are they doing? Are they feeling more liberated without their diapers, or do they look confused and scared? If it's the latter, hold off reverting to the diapers for a day or two. The confusion and fear are only temporary and will ease away once they become more accustomed to the potty. If it doesn't go away after more than a day, and if more accidents involving them pooping and peeing in the house occur, revert them to the diapers momentarily. But since we're taken seven whole days to taper off their diapers, the likelihood of something like that happening is little.

We have discussed a whole week of potty-training. By this time, your child should have a rudimentary grasp of their potty-training process. If they become autonomous after one week, that's all for the better. But if it feels like they need more time, repeat the instructions for week two, and then week three, letting them become more and more autonomous and independent with the progression of each week. That'll be 21 days in total. By the end of those 21 days, your child's habit will have firmly formed, and many accidents will have minimized to being nonexistent. In the end, consult all your notes that you kept in your journal or app and see the progress. Has it been steady or exponential? What went right? What went wrong? Note these down for your next child or for advice to give to another parent.

The only step left is to transition your child from their potty to an adult toilet.

Chapter Ten: From Potty to Adult Toilet

First of all, congratulations on making it to the final chapter of this book. This right here is progress. Now let's address the last stretch, the final hurdle—transitioning from the potty to the adult toilet. After this, there are no more milestones in the potty-training journey to achieve. Let's quickly review what we have done so far. We've gotten your child to ditch their diaper, we've set up their daytime routine on the potty, we've formed their habit, we've formed their nighttime routine, we've covered some basic do's and don'ts, busted some myths, and tackled some potty related problems. All that remains now is how to shift your child from a potty to the toilet.

Presently, the biggest issue you will face is your child's preference for the smaller potty. They are not to blame here, as, in the previous section, we formed their habit of going on the small potty over 21 days. Now they are accustomed to it. The transition can get tricky, just as the transition from diaper to potty was tricky. But you have to stick to the mantra: this too shall pass. It's only natural to ask yourself how long this phase will last. If only there were a concrete number of days to tell you; sorry, that's never the case.

Your inner sleuth might be doing some detective work by checking up on their pooping and peeing patterns, noticing a break you can utilize and introduce them to the grown-up toilet.

You might have noticed something else. While initially, the appeal of the potty was way too high compared to the diapers, now, on the other hand, after having washed and cleaned the potty for almost a month, you've grown tired of it and cannot wait to get rid of it. And the porcelain toilet is right there, just a few feet away. It's almost tempting to put your toddler on it and tell them to go on it. But that's not how you should do it. It can result in you de-establishing all the training process that you so painstakingly undertook.

When will my child stop using the small potty? That's the biggest question in your mind right now, and rightly so, so here's the answer: It all depends on your child, as with all other steps of potty-training. Consider the fact that a month ago, they were still in their diapers, attuned to pooping and peeing while they were standing up, sitting down, lying down, without a worry, without sticking to any schedule. Then, all of a sudden, they were plunged into a regimen where they were forced to sit down on an alien plastic potty, a seat with a hole, and they had to release their pee or poop. Remember, that was quite a bit for them to take in – sometimes, a little too much for them. They barely had any time to acquaint themselves with the plastic potty, and now you're expecting them to make such a huge developmental leap. As with transitioning from diapers to potty, a child will transition from potty to the porcelain toilet at their own pace.

What makes a child potty-trained? Well, if they have less than two pee-related accidents in a single week and no poop-related accidents, a child is considered potty-trained. Is your child potty-trained after their 21-day potty-training regimen?

If so, let's consider their age. What age-bracket are they in? A child at the age of 22 months will have difficulty in maintaining their balance on a regular toilet without the assistance of a toilet seat. They'll also need a stepstool to get up on the toilet. If your toddler's size is too small, they're going to find the toilet too high and scary to sit on.

If that's the case, keep them on the potty and wait for them to grow up a little in size before putting them on the toilet again. There's no rushing this part of the potty-training. It's the last leg of the training. If your child is getting their poop and their pee in the potty, they're doing what you taught them to do, and that's what matters, isn't it? It's not the vessel that matters as much as what they're trained to do.

Bugging your child about it won't do them any good. It'll only make them feel insufficient and lower their self-esteem.

Did you know that pooping and peeing in a squatting position is easier for your child than in a sitting position? It's also more beneficial, health-wise. That's why it's better to let them stick to the potty for a little while longer.

Another crucial factor is the dropdown. Your child has been pooping in the diaper for years. The sensation of pooping in the diapers versus the sensation of pooping in the potty is entirely different. Now add the feeling of pooping in a toilet in the mix. It's another completely alien feeling, one with drop down added. First, let your child get acquainted with using the potty, i.e., with dropping their poop down, then move on to the bigger toilet. This part of the transition should be as gradual as possible.

The Right Age to Transition to the Toilet

The average age at which a child is completely potty trained is 36 months, which, incidentally, is also the age at which they can easily transition to an adult-sized toilet. At three years of age, a child starts going to a preschool or starts spending time at the homes of other kids their age, so using a toilet becomes necessary, as potties won't always be available for them at these places. So, as their parent, you should get them acquainted with using a full-sized toilet at that age. At that age, their bodies are ready, as are their minds. This task will be almost as difficult as getting them to use the potty. You might need to resolve some emotional issues to get them to use the toilet. Fear, for example. Hesitation, anxiety, apprehension, resistance, and familiarity with the potty.

To ease them with the toilet, you can put their potty right next to the toilet. This will familiarize the child with the toilet whenever they use the potty. The next step involves you buying a toilet seat for your child. Add a stool for their feet support. After they have made the shift to the toilet, remove the potty altogether.

Tips to Make the Transition Easier

1. Post-it Notes for Public Bathrooms

Public bathrooms have self-flushing mechanisms that can sometimes scare your child when they auto-flush. To stop them from doing that, you can take post-it notes and put them on the sensors so that they don't flush when your child's poop or pee drops in the bowl. When they are done going, you can remove the post-it note, and the toilet will resume flushing. Simple, yet genius, right?

2. Headphones for Public Bathrooms

Noise-canceling headphones for public bathrooms work wonders for kids who are anxious about the loud noises in public spaces. The loud noises of people, hand-drying machines, doors opening and closing, and traffic can put performance pressure on a child, making it difficult for them to go. By putting noise-canceling headphones on their head and playing their favorite music on it, you can help them alleviate their anxiety, making it easier for them to go to the bathroom.

3. Teaching Them Toilet-Paper Etiquette

Now that they're able to use the toilet on their own, they should be taught basic toilet-paper etiquette. This includes taking two sheets, breaking them off, folding them, placing them on their butt, wiping them twice, folding them again, wiping them again, then disposing of them again in the toilet bowl. This isn't exactly a discrete habit, as it comes under the domain of going to the bathroom. You can teach this to them in tandem with teaching them to go on the potty.

4. Reading Toilet-Training Books with Them

There's an abundance of children-oriented potty-training literature available on Kindle and in paperbacks that you can read with your child as you help them transition from the potty to the toilet. This will both serve to distract them and inform them of their progress.

5. Cleaning Up After Them

Especially after your boys. After your son has started going to the toilet, they'll start observing their elder brothers, their father, their uncles, and other men at the public bathrooms use the toilets and the urinals standing up. They'll want to use it standing up as well. Besides, you'll have trained him to stand up to pee. They will make a mess the first few times when they're using the toilet, but once they've gotten command over their stream, the mess will take care of itself.

6. Decorating their Bathroom

Even though you've helped in this important transition, the fact remains that they're still a child. If their bathroom is decorated colorfully (with their favorite vibrant shades), they're more likely to spend more time in there. But don't go overboard with the decorations, or they may want to spend ALL their time in there! They must learn that their bathroom is a special room with a special purpose.

7. Assisting Them Now and Then

While independence is a huge step for your kid, it's recommended that you keep an eye on them occasionally to see if everything's going okay and if they need any assistance. Sometimes they'll need you to assist them at a public place where they'll be facing potty-resistance, such as a daycare or a public bathroom.

8. Switch the Parents

We've got a confession to make. We were saving the best advice for last. It's this: If you are having a tough time training your toddler, try switching the parent. If you're a mom, try passing on the responsibility baton to daddy, and if you're dad, try handing over the task to mommy dearest. It can make a remarkable difference when these roles are reversed, regardless of where you are at in the potty-training process.

Conclusion

Now that we've covered all the possible theoretical bases about potty-training, where do you go from here? Well, onwards, you go into that great battlefield known as parenting, armed with the weapon of this profound knowledge, onwards unto the breach! Just kidding. You can relax. Much of this information might have felt a lot to take in, especially if you are a first-time parent. Remember that not all of it is applicable all the time. You have to keep applying it day-to-day.

Let's summarize what we learned in a short paragraph, shall we?

First, we learned what the right time to start potty-training is. In this section, we focused on toddler habits, their growth, and the signs that indicated that your child is ready to begin learning how to use the potty. In the next chapter, we debunked some potty-training myths and misconceptions. Further on, we learned how to ditch diapers without the drama. Then we learned the psychology of potty-pooping and how a botched training can lead to negative effects that can last a lifetime. After that, we guided you through using the potty for the first time and how to assist a child if necessary. Then we elaborated on some potty and pooping problems, some minor accidents, the child's stubbornness, their fears, and ways to solve and prevent problems. We discussed the nighttime potty-training method after that, in which we answered questions, such as whether the child should or shouldn't be woken up at night. There's a difference between potty-training girls and boys. We discussed that in an entire chapter. In the second-last chapter, we discussed how to form potty habits and a few other habits that should complement their main habit. Last, we discussed how to transition your child from their potty to the full-grown toilet.

Equipped with this knowledge, you're now able to potty-train your child properly and carefully. We wish you the best of luck!

www.ingramcontent.com/pod-product-compliance
Lightning Source LLC
Chambersburg PA
CBHW070049230426
43661CB00005B/825